James Colyn was born and raised in Canada. He studied journalism there, English Lit somewhere in Michigan, and journalism again somewhere between cyberspace and London. He has worked as an instructor, writer, and editor in Japan since the Showa Era. He currently lives, works, and plays in Sendai, where he runs an outfit called Colingual.

Vocab-ability

James Colyn

VANTAGE PRESS
New York

FIRST EDITION

All rights reserved, including the right of
reproduction in whole or in part in any form.

Copyright © 2002 by James Colyn

Published by Vantage Press, Inc.
516 West 34th Street, New York, New York 10001

Manufactured in the United States of America
ISBN: 0-533-14066-8

Library of Congress Catalog Card No.: 01-126941

0 9 8 7 6 5 4 3 2 1

Contents

Guide to entries v
Stems (a-z) 1-52
Prefixes (a-z) 53-67
Suffixes (a-z) 68-76
Numbers (numerical order) 77-79
Index 81-84

Guide to entries

Roots — The bold selections at the head of each entry are the roots. Although they are derived from Greek or Latin, they are presented here as they are spelled in current English.

Meanings of roots
The meanings of the roots as they are used in current English.

omni– · *all*

omniscient – *all-knowing.*
omnipotent – *all-powerful.*
omnivorous – *eating both meats and vegetables.*
omnipresent – *everywhere, present in all places at one time.*

Students may think that teachers are **omniscient**, but teachers know better than that.
Such **omnivorous** animals will eat anything they can find.
Even after living in the city for years, I can't get used to the **omnipresent** traffic noise.

Sample words
Examples of the roots in commonly used English words, along with their dictionary definitions.

Model sentences — Sample words (in **bold**) used in sentences to give examples of usage.

Thanks to . . .

Mitsuaki and Emiko Usami, for the time and facilities to research and compile the bulk of this work.

Takako Muranaka, for her assistance in composing model sentences.

Mihoko Owada, for her advice and assistance with the layout and design.

Robert Somerville, for finding and correcting my numerous lapses and errors.

My students, for the motivation to complete this work and for their assurances that it was worthwhile.

A

acri · *sharp*
acer · *bitter*

acrid – *bitter, harsh in taste or smell, harsh in language.*
acrimonious – *bitter, hateful.*
acerbic – *sour, caustic, sarcastic.*
exacerbate – *to aggravate, to irritate, to embitter.*

The two presidential candidates engaged in an **acrimonious** debate.
The aging folk singer still sang songs with **acerbic** wit and biting lyrics.
The poverty in that country is **exacerbated** by overpopulation.

---

ag · *urge*
act · *act*

act – *to work, to do, to mimic. a deed.*
agent – *a person who performs a role, a representative.*
activate – *to start, to put into action.*
agenda – *a list of things to do.*
retroactive – *taking effect from a previous date.*

Established writers often hire **agents** to take care of their contractual affairs.
Push that large lever forward to **activate** the 4-wheel drive.
The raise I got with my new contract is **retroactive** to last April 1.

---

agog · *lead*

demagogue – *a leader who appeals to emotion.*
pedagogy – *study of teaching methods.*
synagogue – *a Jewish temple.*

Although the president was popular, many critics denounced him as a **demagogue**.
Prospective teachers should know a little about **pedagogy**.
The **synagogue** is still the center of life in many Jewish communities.

---

agon · *fight*
· *suffer*

antagonist – *an enemy, an opponent.*
protagonist – *a main character, a hero, a leader.*
agony – *pain, torture, anxiety.*

A skilled boxer will feed off the power of his **antagonist**.
Popular movies have strong, moral **protagonists** who viewers can identify with.
Saving Private Ryan was a graphic film portraying the **agony** of war.

---

agr · *field*
agrari
egri

agriculture – *cultivation of fields.*
agrarian – *pertaining to land or farming.*
peregrination – *wandering, traveling from place to place.*
acre – *a unit of area for measuring land, $4,047 m^2$.*

Agricultural societies maintain strong family and community ties.
The economy of that small country is slowly changing from **agrarian** to industrial.
The Zandstra family owns over 10,000 **acres** of fertile farmland.

ali	• other

        alias – a false name.
        alibi – a possible excuse to prove a person's innocence.
        alienate – to estrange, to repulse.

The fugitive signed into the hotel using an **alias**.
The police released the suspect after they confirmed his **alibi**.
Many voters feel **alienated** from politicians.

alter	• other
altr	• change

        alternate – to fluctuate, to switch back and forth.
        alternative – a choice, one of two possible choices.
        alteration – a change.
        altercation – a battle, a heated dispute with another person.
        alter ego – another side of oneself, a close friend.

His unstable character **alternates** between cheerful and moody.
The new fuel will provide an **alternative** to gasoline.
You should make some **alterations** to your text before sending it to a publisher.

am	• love
ami	• friendship
amo	

        amorous – passionate, loving, erotic.
        amiable – friendly, pleasant, agreeable.
        enamor – to inspire with love, to impress.

Maria was a bit suspicious of Andy's **amorous** intentions.
We chatted **amiably** with many old friends at our high-school reunion.
Many of the young female students were **enamored** of their teacher.

ambul	• walk

        amble – to walk slowly.
        somnambulist – a sleep walker.
        perambulate – to stroll, to travel on foot.

Tourists can often be seen **ambling** through the old part of town.
He was so tired that he was moving around like a **somnambulist**.

anim	• mind
	• soul
	• life
	• spirit

        animate – to enliven, to cheer up.
        unanimous – unified, agreeing.
        magnanimous – generous, big-hearted.

Robert was the **unanimous** choice for the Most Valuable Player award.
Computer **animation** has resulted in very realistic-looking creatures in recent films.
The champ showed true **magnanimity** when he agreed to fight his rival again.

annu • *year*
enni
        anniversary – *yearly celebration.*
        annual – *every year.*
        biennial – *every two years.*
        perennial – *long-lasting, endless, throughout the year.*

The family gathered to celebrate Bill and Margaret's 50th wedding **anniversary**.
The union held its **biennial** conference in Kansas City.
You will have a colorful garden every year if you plant these **perennials**.

anthrop • *human*
        anthropology – *study of man's origin, culture, etc.*
        misanthrope – *a hater of mankind.*
        philanthropy – *charity, helping or supporting needy people.*

The university's **Anthropology** Department sponsored a dig at some ruins in Kyoto.
Professor Larsen has a reputation as a **misanthrope**, so students avoid his classes.
Mr Walker, a generous old billionaire, was well-known for his **philanthropy**.

aqua • *water*
aque
        aquarium – *a tank containing marine life.*
        aqueduct – *an artificial waterway.*
        Aquarius – *The Water Carrier (a horoscope sign).*

Doctor Benton's waiting room is very relaxing now that he's installed an **aquarium**.
Ancient Roman **aqueducts** can still be seen in places as far away as Spain.

arbit • *judge*
        arbitration – *mediation, solving of a dispute.*
        arbiter – *a judge, a referee.*
        arbitrary – *indiscriminate, random, inconsistent.*

The company and the union agreed that the dispute should go to **arbitration**.
The company and the union both accepted the old lawyer as the **arbiter** in the dispute.
Police were puzzled by the **arbitrary** nature of the attacks.

arch • *government*
     • *rule*
        monarch – *a sole ruler, such as a king, queen, or emperor.*
        anarchy – *lack of government, chaos.*
        archives – *historical records of a government.*

Prince Charles is set to become the next **monarch** of Great Britain.
The country descended into a state of **anarchy** after the leader was assassinated.
You'll have to go to the government office to consult the **archives**.

aster · *star*
astro

asterisk – *a star-like character, this sign* *.
astronomy – *study of the stars.*
astrology – *study of the horoscope.*

Seiji hopes to become a professor of **astronomy**.
Astrologists claim to be able to predict the future, but all their predictions are vague.
Please check this list for names with **asterisks** behind them.

---

aud · *hear*
aur

inaudible – *incapable of being heard.*
auditorium – *place where speech or music is heard.*
audience – *a group of listeners.*
aural – *pertaining to hearing.*

The quiet woman's voice was virtually **inaudible**.
We entered the **auditorium** and found our seats just before the concert began.
Professor Prange uses both written and **aural** material in her classroom.

---

aux · *increase*
aug · *add*

auxiliary – *additional, extra, supporting.*
augment – *to increase, to strengthen.*
august – *majestic, grand.*

We have to turn on the **auxiliary** heaters during the cold months.
If I don't get a raise, I'll have to find some way to **augment** my income.

B

belli · *war*
bel

rebel – *dissident, agitator. to fight against.*
belligerent – *intimidating, loud, aggressive.*
antebellum – *before the American Civil War.*

The **rebels** has been fighting an insurgent war against the government for many years.
Although Rick is a very friendly person by nature, he is a **belligerent** athlete.
Antebellum mansions in the south are the finest examples of American architecture.

---

ben · *good*
bon

benefactor – *a supporter, a person who does good.*
benevolence – *charity, goodwill.*
bonus – *a reward, a gift.*
benefit – *help, advantage. to help, to improve.*

Gary was supported by an unknown **benefactor** after his parents died.
The immigrants were pleased to be accepted by the **benevolent** country.

One of the **benefits** of working for this company is its health insurance plan.

bibl   • *book*
bibli

    bibliography – *a list of books.*
    bibliophile – *a book lover.*
    Bible – *The Book.*

That history book has a 30-page **bibliography** at the end.
Bibliophiles enjoy lingering in the many book shops on Catharine Street.

bio   • *life*

    biology – *study of living things.*
    biotechnology – *the use of living cells in technology.*
    biography – *a story of a person's life.*
    antibiotic – *a medicine which destroys bacteria.*

Biotechnology has stirred up a lot of controversy recently.
A new **biography** of Robert Kennedy was published last month.
The patient was given **antibiotics** before his operation.

brev   • *short*
bri

    brief – *short.*
    brevity – *shortness.*
    abbreviate – *to shorten.*
    abridge – *to make shorter, to condense.*

Brevity is the soul of wit. (a proverb)
When you take notes, use **abbreviations** and avoid writing complete words.
An **abridged** version of *The Tale of Genji* was published by Odagiri Press.

C

cad   • *fall*
cas

    decadent – *immoral, depraved, degenerate.*
    cadence – *rising and falling sounds, beat, rhythm.*
    cascade – *waterfall.*
    casualty – *a victim, a fatality, a person who has been hurt.*

Underneath the glitter and glamour, Las Vegas is a rather **decadent** place.
The **cadences** and rhythms of Chinese make it one of the most beautiful languages.
The war resulted in thousands of **casualties**.

cap   • *head*

    decapitate – *to cut a person's head off.*
    captain – *a leader.*
    capital – *a major city. first-rate. wealth in the form of money.*
    per capita – *per person, for every person.*

The soldier was **decapitated** by the helicopter's rotor.

The annual **per-capita** income of that third-world country is less than $500.

c a p	• take
c e p	• contain
c i p	
c e i v	

capture – to seize, to take by force.
accept – to adopt, to believe.
susceptible – likely to be influenced or affected.
participate – to take part.
conceive – to imagine, to visualize.
receive – to take, to get.
recipient – a person who gets something, a receiver.

The rebels finally **captured** the city after weeks of intense fighting.
The workers **accepted** the new contract only after striking for three months.
The **recipient** of the Best Actor award gave it to his acting instructor.

c a r n	• meat

carnal – physical, bodily, of the flesh.
incarnation – an extreme example of a type. a birth.
carnivorous – meat-eating.
carnival – a meat festival.

The sex offender couldn't control his **carnal** desires.
Vegetarians believe that man is not a **carnivorous** animal.
He believes that, in a previous **incarnation**, he was the king of a large nation.

c e d	• go
c e s	• move

recede – to go back, withdraw.
antecedent – a preceding event or word.
concede – to yield.
incessant – continual, not stopping.
recession – a slow economy.

After the heavy rains stopped, the floodwaters started to **recede**.
The **antecedents** of the horse crossed a land bridge into Asia millions of years ago.
Rudy is not only a chain-smoker, but also an **incessant** coffee drinker.

c e l e r	• speed

accelerate – to go faster.
decelerate – to slow down.
celerity – swiftness, quickness.

With the IT revolution, the country experienced a period of **accelerated** growth.
Careful drivers will always **decelerate** well before making a turn.

c e n d	• fire
c a n d	• shine

incendiary – a weapon which can causes large fires.
incense – to fire up, to make angry.
incandescent – giving off light after being heated.

The rioters threw homemade **incendiary** bombs at the government buildings.
She was so **incensed** after their argument that she slammed the door in his face.
Incandescent lights are not as efficient as fluorescent lights.

centri • *center*
centr • *middle*

    centrifugal – *moving away from the center.*
    centripetal – *moving towards the center.*
    centralize – *to focus on the center.*

Centrifugal force kept the water from spilling as he swung the bucket over his head.
Japan has a **centralized** government, so the regional governments have little power.

cern • *separate*
cri

    discern – *to perceive, to distinguish.*
    discrimination – *bias, prejudice. awareness, insight.*
    discrete – *separate, distinct.*

It was so foggy we could hardly **discern** the buildings across the road.
We find examples of racial **discrimination** in even the most tolerant societies.
The entire process can be divided into several **discrete** stages.

chrom • *color*

    achromatic – *colorless, black or white.*
    monochrome – *having one color.*
    chromatic – *having bright colors, pertaining to color.*

The exhibition featured a number of **monochrome** paintings.
All household appliances used to be **achromatic**.

chron • *time*

    chronology – *a time table of events.*
    anachronism – *something out of time sequence.*
    synchronize – *to set or occur at the same time.*

The collection of paintings is displayed in **chronological** order.
A motorcycle in ancient Rome was one of the **anachronisms** presented in the film.
Let's **synchronize** our watches now, and meet outside the cafe at exactly 6 o'clock.

cid • *cut*
cis • *kill*

    incision – *a surgical cut.*
    scissors – *a cutting tool.*
    homicide – *murder, killing of a human.*
    suicide – *killing oneself.*
    infanticide – *killing a baby.*

The surgeon made an long **incision** on the left side of the patient's torso.
The young mother was mistakenly charged with **infanticide** after her child died.
The **suicide** rate increased as the recession dragged on into its fifth year.

circum · *around*

circumstance – *condition, environment, situation.*
circumnavigate – *to sail around the world.*
circumspect – *cautious, careful, looking around.*
circumlocution – *unclear, indirect speech, talking in circles.*

Some people think that Columbus was the first person to **circumnavigate** the globe.
If you're going to search through those secret files, you should be very **circumspect**.
The journalists were confused by the politician's **circumlocution**.

---

cit · *call*
citat

incite – *to stir up, to encourage, to instigate.*
excite – *to arouse, to provoke, to fascinate.*
recite – *to narrate, to say again.*

The leaders of that right-wing group are notorious for **inciting** violence.
The young pupil got up in front of the crowd and **recited** the poem he had written.
The children were very **excited** when they heard that the circus was coming to town.

---

civi · *citizen*

civilization – *society of citizens, culture.*
civilian – *member of a community, not soldiers.*
civil – *pertaining to citizens or community. polite.*

The Romans introduced **civilization** to large parts of Western Europe.
Relations between soldiers from the army base and **civilians** in the town are tense.
He was upset about the situation, but he responded **civilly** and accepted the offer.

---

clam · *cry out*
claim

clamor – *noisy shouting, loud demands.*
acclaim – *praise, verbal approval.*
proclaim – *to announce, to broadcast, to declare.*

The **clamor** of the crowd continued into the early hours of the morning.
Her latest novel has received great critical **acclaim**.
Immediately after the earthquake, the governor **proclaimed** a state of emergency.

---

clar · *clear*

clarify – *to make clear, to explain.*
declare – *to state clearly, to announce.*
clairvoyance – *fortune-telling, clear vision.*

You'll have to **clarify** your story if you want everyone to understand it.
The president **declared** that he would not resign.
The fortune teller claimed to be **clairvoyant**.

---

clud · *close*
clus · *shut*

conclude – *to finish, to close down.*
secluded – *isolated, closed off, deserted.*
exclusive – *closed off, private.*

recluse – *a hermit, a person who likes to be alone.*
claustrophobia – *fear of closed spaces.*

He has **claustrophobia**, so he has only un-curtained windows in his house.
Reverend Muirhead **concluded** the meeting with a prayer.
We'll never get into that **exclusive** club unless we're invited by someone.

clin	• *bend*
	• *lean*

recline – *to lean back, to relax.*
decline – *to slope downwards, to lessen.*
inclination – *a tendency.*

She sat down gracefully on the sofa and **reclined** against the plush back.
The crime rate of that city has **declined** in the past few years.
It seems as if many young people have an **inclination** towards violent behavior.

cogni	• *know*
	• *learn*

recognize – *to realize, to know, to distinguish.*
incognito – *disguised.*
cognition – *perception, the process of knowing.*
connoisseur – *an expert, a critic, an epicure.*

I **recognize** your face, but I can't remember your name.
The famous movie actor walked through the crowded mall **incognito**.
Scientists and psychologists are studying how the brain functions in **cognition**.

cord	• *heart*
cor	• *mind*
cour	

accord – *agreement.*
cordial – *friendly, polite.*
discord – *disagreement, incongruity.*
courage – *bravery.*
discourage – *to dishearten, to stifle enthusiasm.*

The peace **accord** between the Palestinians and the Israelis was soon broken.
The guests were greeted **cordially** at the entrance and escorted into the dining room.
After failing the test, Mike became **discouraged** and soon quit studying.

corp	• *body*
corpor	
corpus	

incorporate – *to organize into a body, to include.*
corporeal – *pertaining to the body, not spiritual.*
corpse – *a dead body.*
esprit de corps – *spirit of loyalty among members of a group.*

Let's **incorporate** the company logo in the design of our new letterhead.
Homicide detectives found an unidentified **corpse** in the trunk of a car on Main Street.
That company's success is due partly to the **esprit de corps** of its employees.

cosm   • *universe*
          • *world*

        microcosm – *a small model of the world, a small world.*
        cosmology – *scientific study of the universe.*
        cosmopolitan – *worldly, sophisticated, international.*

A Japanese office is a **microcosm** of Japanese society.
While retaining its distinctive Thai flavor, Bangkok is definitely a **cosmopolitan** city.
Stephen Hawking's book, *A Brief History of Time*, stimulated interest in **cosmology**.

---

cresc   • *grow*
cre

        increase – *to become larger, to grow in size.*
        decrease – *to become smaller, to become less.*
        crescendo – *an increase in volume in music or noise.*
        accretion – *gradual growth or increase.*

The population of that town **decreased** to half its former size after the factory closed.
Coral reefs form slowly over many years by a process of **accretion**.
The audience was awed when the entire band reached a **crescendo** simultaneously.

---

cred   • *believe*
        • *trust*

        incredible – *unbelievable, astonishing.*
        credibility – *dependability, trustworthiness.*
        credence – *believability.*
        creed – *a statement of beliefs, religion.*

Ripley's "Believe It Or Not" featured many **incredible** but true stories.
Bush lost the election because voters doubted his **credibility**.
Most Protestant churches have similar **creeds**, but they differ on the interpretations.

---

crypt   • *secret*

        encrypt – *to put into code, to make secret.*
        cryptonym – *a secret name.*
        cryptic – *mysterious, secret.*
        crypto-fascist – *secretly fascist.*

Microsoft has **encrypted** its software to safeguard its code.
The newspaper received a **cryptic** letter yesterday from an anonymous source.
Left-wing activists have accused that magazine of being **crypto-fascist**.

---

culp   • *blame*

        culprit – *a guilty person.*
        culpable – *responsible for an error, guilty.*
        exculpate – *to absolve, to free from guilt.*

The police worked night and day until they had arrested the **culprit**.
The leader of the criminal group refused to admit **culpability**.
The suspect was **exculpated** after his alibi was confirmed.

---

cur   • *attention*
        • *care*

        curator – *a person in charge of a place.*

curious – *interested, inquisitive, strange.*
secure – *safe.*

The **curator** of the museum resigned after the second masterpiece was stolen.
Children tend to be **curious** about most new things.
Your valuables will be **secure** if you leave them at the Front Desk.

cur • *flow*
curs • *run*
cours

    current – *a flow, movement.*
    concur – *to agree.*
    cursory – *brief, quick, speedy.*
    excursion – *a journey.*
    precursor – *a forerunner.*

The swift **current** of the river soon carried the boat far downstream.
Jerry was hired after only a **cursory** interview with the manager.
Large desktop computers were the **precursors** of today's notebook computers.

D

dat • *give*
dit

    data – *facts, statistics.*
    mandate – *a command.*
    tradition – *a custom, a practice handed down to offspring.*

Data collected by the government shows that the economy is recovering.
The conservative leader claimed that he had a **mandate** to increase defense spending.
They have kept up the **tradition** of celebrating the harvest time.

deb • *owe*

    debt – *borrowed money, something owed.*
    indebtedness – *obligation.*
    debit – *a record of money taken out of an account.*

After receiving student loans for 6 years, I was $30,000 in **debt**.
Thank you for your valuable assistance. I will always be **indebted** to you.
Your account has $500 on the **debit** side and $150 on the credit side.

dem • *people*

    democracy – *government by the people.*
    demographics – *features of the human population of an area.*
    epidemic – *widespread disease.*
    endemic – *native, indigenous.*

Russia adopted **democracy** after the collapse of communism.
MacDonald's will open a restaurant only after studying the **demographics** of an area.
The AIDS **epidemic** has spread to every country on the planet.

dent   · *tooth*
dont

dentures – *false teeth.*
dentist – *a tooth doctor.*
orthodontist – *a dentist who works with teeth structure.*
trident – *a three-pronged fork.*

My grandpa puts his **dentures** in a glass of water on his bedside table at night.
Gerine made an appointment with the **dentist** when she got a toothache.
The **orthodontist** suggested that I wear braces for several months.

---

derm   · *skin*

epidermis – *the outer layer of skin.*
pachyderm – *an elephant, a thick-skinned quadruped.*
dermatology – *study of the skin and its disorders.*
hypodermic – *a syringe to inject drugs under the skin.*

This moisturizing lotion is good for the **epidermis**.
You should see a **dermatologist** about your dry skin.
The doctor picked up the **hypodermic** needle and gave the patient an injection.

---

di   · *day*
diurn

diary – *a daily book.*
diurnal – *pertaining to daytime.*
meridian – *the midday line, a north-south line on a map.*

The kangaroo is a **diurnal** animal.
The prime **meridian** passes through Greenwich, England, at O°.

---

dic   · *say*
dict

diction – *speech, manner of speaking.*
predict – *to tell the future.*
contradict – *to disagree, to challenge, to say the opposite.*
abdicate – *to resign, to step down.*

Professor Armstrong was known on campus for his fine **diction**.
The vice-president **contradicted** the president when commenting on the economy.
My financial advisor correctly **predicted** the crash of the stock market.

---

doc   · *teach*
doct

doctor – *a highly educated man.*
indoctrinate – *to educate, to persuade.*
doctrine – *a set of beliefs or teachings.*
docile – *meek, easily teachable.*

The citizens of that country were **indoctrinated** in the ruling party's ideology.
Castro is still a firm believer in the Marxist **doctrine** of continual revolution.
Mrs Shanley's daughters are quiet and **docile**, but her sons are noisy and aggressive.

dom · *rule*
domin · *govern*

dominate – *to have power over.*
kingdom – *land ruled by a king.*
domain – *a field of activity, land ruled by someone.*

Michael Jordan **dominated** the NBA for many years.
The United **Kingdom** actually consists of four countries ruled by England.
Picasso was one of the **dominant** figures in the **domain** of modern art.

duc · *lead*
duct · *bring*

conduct – *to lead, to guide.*
abduct – *to kidnap.*
education – *learning, experience, training.*
aqueduct – *an artificial waterway.*

The policeman had to **conduct** traffic when the signal lights malfunctioned.
The young child was **abducted** while her mother was in the store.
Roman **aqueducts** can still be seen in parts of Europe far from Italy.

dur · *hard*
 · *lasting*

durable – *strong, rugged.*
endurance – *perseverance, persistence.*
duration – *the time during which something lasts.*

That toy company has succeeded by making strong and **durable** toys.
Mountain climbing is a sure test of a person's **endurance**.
Newspapers were not allowed to report the case for the **duration** of the trial.

dynam · *strength*
 · *power*

dynamic – *powerful, active, vigorous.*
dynamo – *a machine that produces electrical power.*
aerodynamics – *the science of air power.*

Voters always seem to be attracted to energetic and **dynamic** leaders.
Little Bobby is a kid **dynamo**; not even his father can keep up with him.
The Wright brothers were the first to put **aerodynamic** principles to practical use.

E

ego · *self*

egoist – *a person who is interested in himself.*
egotist – *an overly self-centered person.*
egocentric – *selfish, self-centered.*

Walter is an **egotist** who never stops talking about himself and his accomplishments.
Most people avoid Sean because of his **egocentric** behavior.

equi · *equal*
equa

    equilibrium – *balance, stability.*
    equivalent – *equal, synonymous, corresponding.*
    adequate – *sufficient, enough.*

I'd advise you not to buy any more stocks until prices reach a state of **equilibrium**.
Ten kilometers is **equivalent** to six miles.
Many people throughout the world do not get **adequate** food or nutrition.

erg · *work*
org

    energy – *power, fuel.*
    organ – *a structure which works or performs a certain function.*
    metallurgy – *the art of working metal.*

My grandfather still has lots of **energy** and enthusiasm at 70.
The accident victim injured some muscles and several of his **organs**.

err · *wander*

    error – *a mistake, a defect.*
    erratic – *not constant, unbalanced, inconsistent.*
    knight-errant – *a wandering knight.*
    aberration – *a delusion, a fantasy, insanity.*

The editor found many **errors** in the new writer's articles.
Doctors were worried about the patient's **erratic** heartbeat.
Those strange artists were accused of homosexuality and other sexual **aberrations**.

esth · *perceive*
aesth · *feel*

    esthetic – *tasteful, artistic, stylish.*
    esthetics – *study of the principles of beauty.*
    anesthetic – *pain killer.*

The interior designers chose that furniture only for its **esthetic** appeal.
Both art students and philosophy students have enrolled in the **Esthetics** course.
The dentist gave the patient a local **anesthetic** before starting work on her teeth.

ev · *time*
    · *age*
    · *era*

    longevity – *age, length of life, length.*
    medieval – *pertaining to the Middle Ages.*
    primeval – *prehistoric, ancient, instinctive.*

The sociologist commented on the **longevity** of Scandinavians.
We visited a **medieval** castle in the English countryside.
Conservationists have campaigned to protect the **primeval** forests from loggers.

F

fac · *face*

facsimile – *an exact copy, a method of transmitting copies.*
facade – *the front of a building, a superficial appearance.*
facetious – *amusing, not serious, sarcastic.*
multi-faceted – *having many facets, aspects, or talents.*

They seemed like a happily married couple, but that was only a **facade**.
The teacher reprimanded the students for their **facetious** remarks.
She is a **multi-faceted** performer who can take on any role in any kind of theater.

fac · *make*
fact · *shape*
fect · *operate*
fic · *act*

factory – *a place where things are made.*
fiction – *a made-up story.*
affect – *to influence, to cause to change.*
manufacture – *to produce, to make by hand.*
infect – *to make sick, to make dirty.*
effect – *a product, a result.*

Sometimes truth is stranger than **fiction**.
The children were seriously **affected** by their parents bitter divorce.
The police clamp-down had a noticeable **effect** in reducing the crime rate.

fall · *wrong*
fals · *deceive*

false – *not true.*
infallible – *perfect, incapable of being wrong.*
fault – *responsibility, a defect, a mistake.*

The president announced that rumors of his resignation were **false**.
She is a very skilled technician with years of experience, but she's not **infallible**.
The error which caused the explosion was the **fault** of the lead engineer.

fer · *bring*
     · *carry*

transfer – *to bring from one place to another.*
coniferous – *bearing cones (as pine trees).*
infer – *to understand, to assume the meaning.*
refer – *to direct attention somewhere, to relate to something.*

Mr Tanaka was **transferred** to the branch office in Hiroshima.
Astronomers correctly **inferred** that there was a planet circulating that distant star.
If you can't determine the meaning of the word from context, **refer** to a dictionary.

ferv · *boil*
      · *hot*

fervent – *intense, sincere, impassioned.*
fervor – *enthusiasm, passion.*
effervescent – *bubbly, lively, sparkling.*

They have always been **fervent** supporters of human rights.
That group of outsiders has been ridiculed for its religious **fervor**.
The runners were given large cups of **effervescent** mineral water at the finish line.

---

fid · *trust*
fidel · *faith*

confide – *to entrust, to believe in, to tell a secret.*
fidelity – *faithfulness, loyalty, devotion.*
high fidelity – *faithful reproduction of sound.*
affidavit – *an official declaration of truth, a written oath.*
bona fie – *real, genuine, authentic.*

The senator **confided** to us that he could no longer support the president.
New immigrants must promise **fidelity** to the laws and leaders of the country.
The defendant gave a sworn **affidavit** to his lawyer.

---

fin · *end*
 · *limit*

finite – *limited, having an end.*
infinite – *unlimited, eternal, extremely great in amount.*
confine – *to limit, to restrict, to restrain.*

The supply of oil is **finite**, so we must look for alternative sources of energy.
The sky is filled with an **infinite** number of stars.
John was **confined** to his bed for a month after his legs were injured in the accident.

---

firm · *support*
 · *strong*

confirm – *to verify, to establish.*
affirm – *to promise, to assert, to state strongly.*
infirm – *weak, sick.*

The airline has **confirmed** the fact that all the passengers died in the crash.
The candidate **affirmed** his plan to decrease taxes for the richest citizens.
My grandparents moved into a retirement home after becoming weak and **infirm**.

---

flam · *burn*
flagr · *fire*

inflammable – *burnable, combustible.*
inflammatory – *heated, causing anger or hostility.*
flamboyant – *showy, bold, conspicuous.*
flagrant – *shocking, outrageous, scandalous.*

The public was outraged by the **inflammatory** comments of the congressman.
The **flamboyant** pop star was known more for his dress than for his music.
The raid by the FBI was a **flagrant** violation of our constitutional rights.

---

flect · *bend*
flex · *turn*

reflect – *to bounce back, to mirror.*
flexible – *bendable, versatile.*
deflect – *to turn aside, to bend away.*

I was momentarily blinded by the sun **reflecting** off the windows of the building.
Since that material is strong but **flexible**, it has many uses.
The scandal-plagued minister **deflected** accusations about his behavior.

flu	• *flow*
fluct	
flux	

fluid – *a liquid, a substance which flows. liquid, watery.*
fluency – *flowing, graceful speech.*
influence – *to effect, to convince, to control.*
influx – *movement inwards.*
fluctuation – *a wave, a pulse, a vibration.*

She became **fluent** in French within three years of moving to Montreal.
The Velvet Underground has had a great **influence** on music since the 1970s.
While on a strict diet, I've learned to ignore tiny **fluctuations** in my weight.

foli • *leaf*

foliage – *leaves, greenery.*
portfolio – *a collection of pages, a file.*
defoliant – *a chemical which kills leaves.*

That mountain village is beautiful when surrounded by colorful autumn **foliage**.
Applicants should take a **portfolio** of their work to the interview.
The US Army sprayed tons of **defoliant** over the Vietnamese countryside.

form • *shape*
• *figure*
• *model*

formation – *shaping, creation.*
formula – *a method, recipe, procedure.*
conform – *to correspond, to agree.*
deformed – *distorted, misshapen.*

The Prime Minister announced the **formation** of a new government.
Mediators announced plans for a new **formula** to bring peace to the region.
Aggressive players will have difficulty **conforming** to the new, stricter rules.

fort • *strong*

fortify – *to strengthen.*
fortitude – *persistence, stamina, endurance.*
forte – *strong point.*
comfort – *to ease, to relieve, to support.*

The army **fortified** their position as the enemy approached.
Margaret is a skilled pianist, but creativity is definitely not her **forte**.
Eileen's family and friends tried to **comfort** her after her terrible experience.

fortun • *chance*
• *luck*

fortunate – *lucky.*
fortune teller – *a person who predicts future events.*
fortune – *luck, wealth, riches.*

17

misfortune – *bad luck.*

We were very **fortunate** to find our way back to camp before dark.
Steve made a **fortune** in the first few years of the Internet boom.
He had the **misfortune** to lose most of his money soon after investing it in stocks.

frag
fract
· *break*

fragile – *breakable.*
fracture – *a break. to break.*
fragment – *a broken piece.*

You should write "**Fragile**, handle with care" on all boxes with breakable items.
Bill **fractured** his leg in the first football game of the season.
My mother's favorite vase fell to the floor and broke into **fragments**.

fratri
frater
· *brother*

fraternal – *brotherly, showing strong friendship.*
fratricide – *killing one's brother.*
fraternity – *a college dorm for men, friendship.*

We tried to overcome our differences through **fraternal** discussions.
Everyone needs the **fraternity** of friends and colleagues to get along in society.

front
· *face*
· *fore*

confront – *to face directly, to challenge.*
affront – *an insult, dishonor.*
frontier – *a border, the farthest point of advance.*

The slowing economy has **confronted** the government with a major predicament.
He took my criticism of his music as a personal **affront**.
The **frontier** of American expansion moved rapidly westward as immigrants poured in.

fug
· *escape*
· *flee*

fugitive – *a person who is escaping.*
refugee – *an exile, a person who flees to a safe place.*
refuge – *a safe place, a shelter.*
subterfuge – *deceit, dishonesty.*

Police arrested the **fugitives** after they had been on the run for two weeks.
Canada has been known as a prime destination for **refugees** from war-torn countries.
The mountain climbers found **refuge** from the storm in a tiny cave.

fund
· *bottom*

fundamental – *basic.*
found – *to establish, to start.*
profound – *deep, serious, important.*

Students must first learn the **fundamental** elements of the language.
He **founded** his company while he was still in college.

A **profound** sadness swept the nation after the death of the beloved poet.

fus • *melt*
• *pour*
   confuse – *to complicate, to perplex, to bewilder.*
   fusion – *connection, cohesion, blend.*
   infuse – *to fill, to permeate.*

I was **confused** by the wide range of computers available.
Her music is a **fusion** of jazz and Cuban melodies.
A sense of anticipation **infused** the area before the celebrity appeared.

G

gam • *marriage*
   monogamy – *marriage to one person.*
   bigamy – *marriage to two people at the same time.*
   polygamy – *having many spouses at the same time.*
   amalgamate – *to unite, to consolidate.*

Monogamy is the norm in most societies, but some groups still practice **polygamy**.
Those three companies have decided to **amalgamate** into one large corporation.

gen • *class*
gener • *kind*
  • *race*
   homogeneous – *having the same characteristics, pure.*
   genocide – *killing of an entire race of people.*
   gender – *classification, sex (i.e., male or female).*
   genre – *type, kind, style.*

Japan is a relatively **homogeneous** society, with only a small percentage of foreigners.
The Nazis were not the only ones to carry out a policy of **genocide**.
Some women feel that they are discriminated against because of their **gender**.

geo • *earth*
   geologist – *a scientist who studies the earth.*
   geography – *study of the features of the earth.*
   geocentric – *having the earth at the center.*
   geothermal – *pertaining to the internal heat of the earth.*

Geologists predict that an earthquake will occur here in the next 10-20 years.
The Copernican revolution overturned the idea of a **geocentric** universe.
The Ministry of Energy has tried to promote the use of **geothermal** energy.

gnosc • *know*
   diagnose – *to analyze, to determine by examination.*
   agnostic – *a person who rejects any knowledge of God.*
   prognosis – *a prediction, a forecast.*

The doctor **diagnosed** her illness as leukemia.
Rev Smith was thrown out of the church for expressing his **agnostic** beliefs.
According to the doctor's **prognosis**, Mr Ball will be out of the hospital in a month.

grad · *go*
gress · *stage*
· *degree*

gradual – *slow, step by step, in stages.*
progress – *to advance, to proceed.*
degrade – *to lower in value, to insult.*
aggressive – *assertive, forceful, offensive.*
transgression – *a sin, a crime.*
degree – *a level, a grade, a step.*

The city experienced a **gradual** increase in population as industries moved in.
Only **aggressive** salesman will be able to succeed in this business.
After **graduating** with a Master's **Degree**, you'll find manual labor to be **degrading**.

graph · *writing*
gram

epigram – *a short, witty statement.*
autograph – *a person's signature.*
paragraph – *a section of writing.*

Oscar Wilde had a special flair for composing **epigrams**.
The star baseball player spends hours after each game signing **autographs**.
The beginning of each **paragraph** should be indented.

grat · *thankful*
grac · *pleasing*

congratulate – *to praise, to salute, to wish joy.*
gratitude – *thankfulness.*
ingrate – *a thankless person.*
grateful – *thankful.*

Everyone **congratulated** them on getting married.
We have a deep sense of **gratitude** to you for helping us through our troubles.
"I'd be **grateful** if you'd just initial my first name," Tom Hanks said ominously.

grav · *heavy*

aggravate – *to make worse.*
gravity – *seriousness. the attraction of physical objects.*
grief – *sadness.*

His obesity was **aggravated** by his constant beer drinking.
Most of the people did not understand the **gravity** of the situation until it was too late.
The entire nation was **grief**-stricken after the disaster killed thousands.

greg · *group*
· *herd*
· *flock*

gregarious – *sociable, neighborly, friendly.*
aggregate – *total, sum. grouped together.*
egregious – *noticeably bad, outrageous.*
congregation – *a group of people gathered together.*

They are **gregarious** children who are always surrounded by friends and playmates.
Economists based their predictions on the growth of **aggregate** demand.
China was accused of committing **egregious** abuses of human rights.

gru	• agree

congruence – similarity, correspondence.
incongruous – inharmonious, out-of-place.

The friction resulted from the lack of **congruence** among the various groups.
The tiny wooden church looked **incongruous** in the midst of the skyscrapers.

H

habit	• reside
	• live

inhabitant – a resident, a tenant, a citizen.
habitat – surroundings, environment, atmosphere.
habitable – good enough to live in.

The **inhabitants** of that building are all crack addicts who are living there illegally.
Most animals have difficulty living outside of their native **habitat**.
We'll have to do a lot of work to make this old house **habitable**.

heli	• sun
helio	

heliocentric – having the sun as the center.
helium – a light gas found in the sun's atmosphere.

Some Bible-banging fanatics refuse to accept that our solar system is **heliocentric**.
Thousands of balloons filled with **helium** floated out of the stadium.

her	• stick
hes	

coherent – understandable, logical.
adhere – to stick, to be devoted.
adhesive – glue, cement, or other sticky substance.
hesitate – to stay in one spot, to not move forward.

The editor presented a very **coherent** argument for not splitting infinitives.
We used a very strong **adhesive** to attach the shelf to the wall.
She **hesitated** to make any career changes during the recession.

homo	• man
homi	• human

Homo sapiens – human beings.
homicide – murder, killing of a human.
hominoid – manlike, resembling a human.

There are minor differences between **Homo sapiens** and monkeys; their brains.
The **homicide** department started investigating after a body was found by the river.

hosp • host
• guest

hospitality – *kindness to guests.*
inhospitable – *unfriendly.*
hospice – *a home for people who are dying.*

We gave our hosts some fruit to thank them for their **hospitality**.
The Sahara Desert is one of Earth's most **inhospitable** regions.
The sick old man moved into a **hospice**, where he would be well taken care of.

hydro • water

hydroelectricity – *electricity generated from falling water.*
hydroponics – *cultivation of plants in water.*
hydraulics – *power produced by pressure from liquid.*

Niagara Falls provides **hydroelectricity** to large areas of both Canada and the US.
Hydroponics is used to grow not only flowers and vegetables, but also marijuana.
The implement runs on **hydraulic** power from a tractor.

hyper • above
• beyond
• too much

hyperactive – *overly active, having too much energy.*
hypertension – *a state of high emotional tension.*
hyperbole – *exaggeration.*
hypersensitive – *easily offended, sensitive to drugs.*

A bad diet can result in **hyperactivity** in children.
Many hard-working businessman end up victims of **hypertension**.
The press releases calling him the greatest writer in the country were only **hyperbole**.

hypo • under
• less

hypodermic – *a syringe to inject drugs under the skin.*
hypothermia – *very low body temperature.*
hypothesis – *an assumption, a guess.*

To fight the spread of AIDS, heroin addicts can now get clean **hypodermic** needles.
After the mountain climbers were rescued, they were treated for **hypothermia**.
Scientists discussed various **hypotheses** to explain the phenomenon.

I

it • trip
itiner • go

exit – *way out.*
itinerary – *plan for a trip.*
transit – *the carrying of goods or people between places.*

The emergency **exit** was blocked by a large old sofa.
After Paris, Rome was the next stop on our **itinerary**.
The order of goods you sent us was damaged somewhere in **transit**.

J

jact · *throw*
ject

    project – *to plan, to extend. a plan.*
    reject – *to refuse, to renounce, to abandon.*
    inject – *to insert, to force in, to inoculate.*
    dejected – *sad, depressed.*

The municipal board approved the **project** to establish a new school.
He got down on his knees and asked her to marry him, but she **rejected** his proposal.
The nurse **injected** the patient with a powerful muscle relaxant.

join · *join*
junct · *unite*

    adjoin – *to touch, to border on, to be next to.*
    junction – *a place where two roads meet.*
    conjunction – *a word which joins two other words together.*
    conjoined – *joined together, not separate.*

I was told to wait for the personnel manager in an **adjoining** office.
You will learn about subordinating **conjunctions** such as 'although' and 'because.'
The **conjoined** twins were separated in a seven-hour operation at the Medical Center.

journ · *day*

    journal – *a daily record of events, a magazine or newspaper.*
    journey – *a trip, (a day's travel).*
    adjourn – *to put off to another day, to postpone.*

I said I wanted to read *The Wall Street Journal*, not your personal **journal**.
He is planning a 6-month **journey** through South-East Asia.
The judge **adjourned** the trial on Thursday afternoon to play a round of golf.

jur · *swear*
jurat · *vow*

    jury – *a group of people sworn to seek the truth.*
    perjury – *false testimony.*
    abjure – *to reject, to renounce.*

The **jury** finally reached a verdict of 'not guilty' after 10 hours of discussion.
All the evidence given by the witness was disregarded after he committed **perjury**.
The prime minister's entire cabinet **abjured** the taking of bribes during the election.

just · *right*
jur · *law*
judg

    injure – *to damage, to harm, to do wrong.*
    adjust – *to change, to make right.*
    justice – *fair treatment, right behavior, the law.*
    judgment – *a decision concerning what is right.*
    jurisdiction – *the right and authority to interpret the law.*

After the mechanic made some **adjustments** to my engine, it runs very smoothly.
Justice was done when the sadistic murderer was sentenced to 50 years.
The case was not under state **jurisdiction**, so it went to a federal court.

juv · *young*
jun

juvenile – *young, immature. youth.*
junior – *a young person, a younger person.*
youth – *a young person, the time when a person is young.*
rejuvenate – *to revive, to make young again.*

Juvenile crime has increased 25% over the last year.
Most people recall the days of their **youth** with nostalgia.
We feel completely **rejuvenated** after our two-week camping trip.

L

labor · *work*

laboratory – *a place where scientific work is done.*
collaborate – *to work together.*
laborious – *difficult, time-consuming.*

The researchers have been working in the **laboratory** for 15 hours now.
Dr Wells and Dr Nakamura **collaborated** on the design of the new engine.
Running the office and advising the sales team is very **laborious** work.

laps · *fall*
· *slip*

collapse – *to fall down, to cave in.*
relapse – *to slip back into a bad state.*
lapse – *a minor slip, a failure.*

The roof **collapsed** under the weight of the snow.
While the drug is effective in the short term, patients may **relapse** after a few weeks.
During surgery, doctors cannot have even the smallest **lapse** of concentration.

later · *side*

lateral – *sideways.*
unilateral – *one-sided.*
bilateral – *two-sided.*
collateral – *secondary, subordinate, parallel.*

The quarterback threw a short **lateral** pass to the running back.
The two nations signed a **bilateral** agreement to reduce greenhouse gas emissions.
Some schools and houses suffered **collateral** damage when the airport was bombed.

lect · *choose*
leg

select – *to choose.*
elect – *to choose, to vote into government.*
neglect – *to ignore, to disregard, to overlook.*
eligible – *available, qualified to be chosen.*

eclectic – *specially selected from various sources.*

Her book was **selected** as the winner of the Pulitzer Prize.
George W Bush is the second son of a former president to be **elected** president.
Bill is a lazy person who often **neglects** his duties.

leg lect	• *read*

> **legible** – *readable.*
> **lecture** – *a speech.*
> **intellectual** – *intelligent, educated, well-read.*
> **legend** – *a story, a written tale.*

She has very **legible** handwriting; it's almost as clear as a printed script.
I fell asleep during Professor Harper's **lecture** on modern drama.
A bad diet can seriously hamper the **intellectual** development of a child.

leg	• *law*

> **legislature** – *a law-making group.*
> **legitimate** – *proper, valid, lawful.*
> **legal** – *authorized, lawful.*
> **legislation** – *a law.*

The Conservative Party forced the bill through the **legislature**.
The emperor was returned to his **legitimate** position as figurehead of the government.
The lawyer recommended that his client take **legal** action against the company.

leo	• *lion*

> **leopard** – *a spotted lion.*
> **leonine** – *like a lion, very hairy.*
> **dandelion** – *a yellow flower (literally, "the lion's tooth).*

Brigitte was seen wearing a beautiful **leopard**-skin coat.
The tall **leonine**, blond-haired man attracted stares as he strolled along the beach.
All the lawns in the suburbs are covered with **dandelions** every spring.

lev	• *light* • *lift*

> **alleviate** – *to ease, to relieve, to lighten.*
> **levitate** – *to rise in the air, to float above the ground.*
> **elevator** – *a carriage which raises people or things.*

Sylvia practiced yoga to **alleviate** her back pain.
The guru was seen **levitating** two or three feet in the air.
Guests are transported to the top of the building by **elevator** in 30 seconds.

lib libr	• *book*

> **library** – *a place containing books, a collection of books.*
> **libretto** – *the text of an opera.*
> **libel** – *slander, defamation by printed words.*

The small university features a 3,000,000-book **library**.

A **libretto** written by Mozart was reportedly found in the archives in Vienna.
Mr Barton sued the newspaper for **libel** after it printed degrading comments about him.

---

liber • *free*
lib
        liberate – *to free, to save.*
        liberal – *free-thinking, tolerant, generous.*
        liberty – *freedom.*
        ad-lib – *to act spontaneously. unrehearsed, spontaneous.*

The animal-rights activists broke into the zoo at night and **liberated** dozens of animals.
Ronald Reagan and George Bush were avowed enemies of **liberals**.
The audience loved it when the comedian ignored the script and began **ad-libbing**.

---

lig • *connect*
    • *tie*
        obligation – *a duty, a responsibility, a commitment.*
        ligament – *tissue connecting bones or holding organs.*
        league – *an alliance, an association.*

You can try this product for 10 days free, with no **obligation** to buy it.
The hockey player suffered torn **ligaments** in his knee after he was tripped.
The National Hockey **League** has decided to add two new teams next year.

---

lingua • *language*
lang • *tongue*
        language – *speech, words, symbols of communication.*
        bilingual – *speaking two languages.*
        linguistics – *study of the way language works.*
        lingua franca – *a common language.*
        lingo – *language, speech (informal).*

Children who grow up in a **bilingual** environment can easily learn a third language.
Linguistic theory is not very useful when it comes to learning a second language.
English is the **lingua franca** of the internet.

---

linqu • *leave out*
lict • *omit*
        delinquent – *careless, undutiful, negligent.*
        relinquish – *to hand over, to abandon, to surrender.*
        derelict – *abandoned, neglected, deserted.*

The **delinquent** borrower had his car repossessed when he failed to repay his loan.
The president of the company has decided to **relinquish** power in favor of his son.
Several homeless people are living in **derelict** buildings beside the tracks.

---

loc • *place*
        location – *a place.*
        locate – *to find, to put somewhere.*
        local – *pertaining to a certain area.*
        dislocate – *to displace, to shift.*

Investigators **located** the missing funds in the home of the company vice president.

Most residents of our town prefer to read the **local** newspaper.
Mike **dislocated** his shoulder when he was tackled on the final play of the game.

log · *speech*
loqu · *word*
locut · *study*

    soliloquy – *a speech by an individual.*
    dialogue – *a conversation between two people.*
    eloquence – *fluent, powerful speech.*
    apology – *a speech in defense of something, an explanation.*
    psychology – *study of the mind and behavior.*
    meteorology – *study of weather.*

Hamlet's **soliloquy** is one of the most well-known passages in all of literature.
The audience was impressed by the **eloquence** of the speaker.
We received a letter of **apology** from the store for the delay in service.

luc · *light*
lum

    illumination – *light, lighting.*
    elucidate – *to enlighten, to clarify, to explain.*
    lucid – *clear, understandable.*
    translucent – *transparent, allowing light to pass through.*

The downtown park is lit up every Christmas season with "White **Illumination**."
A few students stayed after class and asked the instructor to **elucidate** his ideas.
The book is a **lucid** account of the tragic attempt to climb the mountain.

M

man · *hand*
manu

    manufacture – *to produce, to make by hand.*
    manuscript – *hand-written text, a text.*
    emancipate – *to free, to liberate.*
    manual – *by hand. a handbook.*
    manipulate – *to handle, to operate, to control, to exploit.*

The writer sent the **manuscript** of his book to several publishing companies.
Doing **manual** labor is healthier than sitting behind a desk all day.
Politicians always try to **manipulate** the press to their advantage.

mania · *enthusiasm*
    · *madness*

    egomania – *obsession with oneself.*
    megalomania – *obsession with power and wealth.*
    bibliomania – *obsession with books.*
    dipsomania – *an uncontrollable desire to drink alcohol.*

Many famous pop stars suffer from **egomania**.
Like most dictators, Hitler suffered from **megalomania**.
Mr Chadwick swears that he's not an alcoholic, just a helpless victim of **dipsomania**.

maniac · *crazed person*
· *lunatic*

    pyromaniac – *a person who likes to set things on fire.*
    kleptomaniac – *a person who feels compelled to steal.*
    megalomaniac – *a person who desires wealth and power.*
    nymphomaniac – *a woman with uncontrollable sexual desire.*

The young **pyromaniac** was arrested after setting several buildings on fire.
A **kleptomaniac** will steal things even if he can afford to pay for them.
The young porn star made her debut in the film *Diary of a Nymphomaniac*.

---

mar · *sea*

    maritime – *pertaining to seafaring, by the seaside.*
    submarine – *an underwater ship.*
    mariner – *a seaman.*

The coastal towns of Canada's **maritime** provinces are popular vacation spots.
John joined the navy because he wanted to work in a **submarine**.
The old **mariner** had worked on ships for 50 years and sailed across every ocean.

---

mater · *mother*
matr

    maternal – *motherly.*
    maternity – *pertaining to giving birth.*
    matricide – *killing one's mother.*
    matriarch – *a female head of a family or tribe.*
    matrix – *a mold, a form, a formative part.*

Pregnant women will notice changes in their behavior due to their **maternal** instincts.
The nurse transferred to the hospital's **maternity** ward to care for new-born babies.
Rose Kennedy was the **matriarch** of America's most famous family.

---

medi · *middle*
mid · *between*

    medium – *average, standard, in the middle.*
    mediate – *to intervene, to go between, to settle.*
    intermediary – *a middleman, a negotiator.*
    mediocre – *average, sub-par.*

The conflict between the company and the union was **mediated** by Judge Watkins.
The **intermediary** negotiated a truce between the two warring groups.
Although Fred was an honor student in high school, he got **mediocre** grades in college.

---

melior · *better*

    ameliorate – *to improve, to make better.*
    melioration – *change of word meaning to a better one.*
    meliorism – *the doctrine that the world can be improved.*

Our marriage counselor worked hard to **ameliorate** our poor marital situation.
After a century of war and two world wars, few believe in the doctrine of **meliorism**.

memor · *remember*

memory – *the ability to remember, remembered things.*
commemorate – *to honor the memory, to serve as a memorial.*
memorandum – *a written report, a short note.*
memoirs – *an autobiography, a record of a person's life.*

There are many monuments in Washington **commemorating** great American leaders.
The senator submitted a **memorandum** to the committee.
Mr Bowers spent the first few years of his retirement writing his **memoirs**.

ment · *mind*

mental – *psychological, emotional.*
mentality – *mood, feeling, state of mind.*
demented – *mentally ill, crazy, out of one's mind.*

Emphasis on athletics can hamper the **mental** development of young pupils.
Ordinary citizens cannot understand the **mentality** of the revolutionaries.
Some **demented** people still think that communism is a viable political system.

merc · *trade*
· *pay*

commerce – *business, trade.*
merchandise – *goods sold by a trader.*
mercenary – *a soldier who works for pay.*

They established a Chamber of **Commerce** to promote business in the town.
Amazon has huge warehouses stocked with books and other **merchandise**.
True revolutionary soldiers have little respect for **mercenaries**.

meter · *measure*
metr
mens

speedometer – *an instrument to measure speed.*
thermometer – *an instrument to measure temperature.*
metric system – *a system of weights and measures.*
commensurate – *similar in scale, proportional.*

The new model cars all have digital **speedometers**.
America is slowly changing from the Imperial system to the **metric** system.
All employees will get raises **commensurate** with the rising cost of living.

min · *small*
minu · *tiny*

minor – *small, insignificant.*
diminutive – *microscopic, tiny. a nickname.*
minute – *tiny, imperceptible.*

The car was totally wrecked in the accident, but the driver escaped with **minor** injuries.
James prefers the **diminutive** "Jimmy," and does not like to be called "Jim."
Even a **minute** amount of that poison can kill dozens of people.

miser   · *unfortunate*
         · *wretched*

      misery – *prolonged or extreme suffering, wretchedness.*
      miserable – *very unhappy or uncomfortable.*
      miser – *a greedy person, a person who hoards money.*
      commiserate – *to show sympathy for someone.*

These photos of people living in **misery** in the slums of Rio de Janeiro are shocking.
After failing the exam, Maria was **miserable** for weeks.
Her friends **commiserated** with her after she failed the exam.

---

mit   · *send*
miss

      missile – *a rocket, something which is thrown or sent.*
      admit – *to allow in.*
      dismiss – *to send away, to fire.*
      emit – *to send out, to discharge, to radiate.*
      mission – *a job, a task.*

Only 300 people will be **admitted** to the theatre for the preview.
Students may not leave the classroom until they are **dismissed** by the teacher.
Mr Sasaki's old car **emits** lots of smoke and fumes.

---

mob   · *move*
mot
mov

      mobile – *movable, easy to move.*
      remove – *to move out, to take away.*
      commotion – *a disturbance, excitement.*
      motion – *movement.*

Mobile phones became more common after they began offering internet services.
After baking the bread for 30 minutes, **remove** it from the oven.
I woke up because of the **commotion** in the hall outside my bedroom.

---

mod   · *manner*
         · *way*

      model – *a representation, an ideal system.*
      modest – *humble, unpretentious, acting the right way.*
      modulate – *to regulate, to change to a suitable manner.*
      modern – *contemporary, the present way.*

The architect presented a **model** of his design for the new city hall.
Although he's a great player, he is very **modest** about his records and achievements.
The actor was very skilled at **modulating** his voice to suit the role.

---

mon   · *warn*
monit   · *remind*

      admonish – *to warn, to reprimand.*
      premonition – *foreboding, prior warning.*
      monitor – *a computer or TV screen. to observe closely.*

The candidate **admonished** the members of his staff regarding the news leak.

Apparently Kennedy had **premonitions** about going to Dallas on that fateful trip.
The nurse **monitored** the patient's condition throughout the night.

mor · *death*
mort

    mortuary – *a room where dead bodies are kept before burial.*
    moribund – *in bad condition, almost dead.*
    immortal – *eternal, undying.*
    murder – *killing of a person.*

The hospital's **mortuary** was filled to capacity after the earthquake.
The finance minister presented his plan to revive the **moribund** economy.
We studied Shakespeare's **immortal** love story, *Romeo and Juliet*.

morph · *shape*
      · *form*

    anthropomorphic – *having the characteristics of humans.*
    morphology – *study of the form of things.*
    metamorphosis – *a change of form.*
    amorphous – *without form.*

The pantheon of Greek gods is an **anthropomorphic** projection of our own world.
The book helps students learn about the **morphology** of the political system.
In Kafka's book *The Metamorphosis*, the protagonist has become a large insect.

mur · *wall*

    mural – *a large painting on a wall.*
    intramural – *within the bounds of a school or institution.*
    extramural – *outside the boundaries, between schools.*

The artist was commissioned to paint a **mural** on the side wall of the civic center.
All students, regardless of skill, are encouraged to participate in **intramural** sports.

mut · *change*

    mutation – *change.*
    permutation – *a major change, a transformation.*
    mutant – *a changed thing, one different from the parental strain.*

The virus can undergo many **mutations** as it tries to fight off the effects of drugs.
The jazz group remained strong and creative through several **permutations**.
Scientists discovered **mutant** creatures caused by the nuclear disaster at Chernobyl.

N

nasc · *birth*
nat

    innate – *inborn, natural, instinctive.*
    native – *belonging by birth, indigenous.*
    prenatal – *before birth.*
    nascent – *in the process of coming into existence.*

Japanese people have an **innate** sense of politeness. And their Emperor is divine.
He is a **native** of Canada, but he has lived most of his life in America.

The **nascent** internet economy made many people rich in the late 1990s.

nav
naut
• *ship*

navigate – *to sail a ship or airplane.*
circumnavigate – *to sail around the world.*
naval – *pertaining to ships and sailing.*
nautical – *pertaining to ships and sailing.*
astronaut – *a space traveler.*

Mr Perez plans to quit his job, buy a small boat, and **circumnavigate** the globe.
Frances decided to go to the **naval** academy, not to university.
The **astronauts** made it safely back to earth after their voyage to the moon.

neg
• *deny*

negative – *"no," "not," pessimistic.*
negate – *to nullify, to void, to neutralize.*
neglect – *to ignore, to disregard, to overlook.*

Sandra has a **negative** outlook on life and a very unpleasant personality.
The people rioted after the dictator **negated** the results of the election.
The teacher had **neglected** to tell us about the test, so it was postponed till next week.

nihil
• *nothing*

annihilate – *to destroy completely, to demolish.*
nihilism – *total rejection of laws, a doctrine that denies truth.*
nihilist – *a person who denies all authority.*

The bombing **annihilated** several towns and villages in the area.
The leader of the anarchist group preached **nihilism** to his followers.

nom
nym
• *name*

nomenclature – *a system for naming things.*
nominate – *to name, to select, to vote for.*
anonymous – *nameless, unknown, unnamed.*
synonymous – *identical, closely related, equivalent.*
acronym – *a word composed of the initial letters of a phrase.*

Some say Hillary will be the first woman **nominated** as a presidential candidate.
The money for the project was donated by an **anonymous** benefactor.
Paris is **synonymous** with high fashion and fine food.

nounce
• *tell*

announce – *to declare publicly, to broadcast.*
pronounce – *to articulate a word, to declare officially.*
renounce – *to reject, to disown.*
denounce – *to criticize severely, to accuse.*

The Olympic Committee **announced** that Toronto would host the next summer games.
The Socialist Party decided to **renounce** Marxism after the Soviet Union collapsed.
Most newspapers **denounced** the government's decision to raise taxes.

nov · *new*

innovation – *a new development.*
novelty – *something new, different, and unusual.*
novice – *a beginner.*

The computer mouse was one of the most useful **innovations** in the industry.
Only a few years ago, the cell phone was still a **novelty**.
I'll need a lot of assistance at my new job, because I'm still a **novice**.

nur · *nourish*
nurt
nutr

nurse – *a person who helps another become healthy.*
nutrient – *food, something which provides nourishment.*
nutrition – *the process of using food for growth. food.*
nurture – *to make grow, to educate, to train.*

You should eat a proper diet providing vitamins, minerals, and other **nutrients**.
Many poor children suffer a serious lack of **nutrition**.
The festival was established to **nurture** promising young musicians from the region.

O

oper · *work*

operate – *to work, to direct.*
cooperation – *working together.*
inoperable – *impossible to be operated on.*

It will take at least a month for you to learn how to **operate** this machine.
Cooperation with foreign countries is necessary for the development of our economy.
The doctor determined that the patient's tumor was **inoperable**.

optic · *vision*
opto

optician – *a person who makes eyeglasses.*
optometrist – *an eye doctor.*
optics – *study of light and vision.*

After the **optometrist** checked my vision, I went to the **optician** to get new glasses.
The field of fiber **optics** has grown rapidly along with the IT revolution.

optim · *best*

optimism – *hope or belief in the best result.*
optimist – *a person who believes all will work out well.*
optimize – *to make the best use of.*

The salesmen expressed **optimism** that the new products would sell well.
Jack is an eternal **optimist**; it seems as if nothing depresses him.
You can **optimize** your computer by installing the new Mac OS-X operating system.

orn · *furnish*

    adorn – *to beautify, to decorate.*
    ornament – *decoration.*
    unadorned – *simple, plain.*

They **adorned** the walls of their new home with paintings by Susan Schmalz.
Let's get the Christmas tree out and put the **ornaments** on tonight.
The dining room was a simple, **unadorned** room, with pastel walls and plain furniture.

ortho · *straight*
     · *correct*

    orthodox – *traditional, strict, correct.*
    orthography – *correct spelling.*
    orthodontist – *a dentist who deals with irregular teeth.*

Most **orthodox** doctors do not practice holistic treatment or give herbal medicine.
The **orthography** of American English differs slightly from that of British English.
The **orthodontist** suggested that the child wear braces on his teeth for a year.

P

pac · *peace*
pax

    pacify – *to make peaceful.*
    pacific – *peaceful.*
    pacifist – *a person opposed to war.*
    Pax Americana – *peace imposed by America on others.*

The umpire tried to **pacify** the irate batter after he was hit by a wild pitch.
Although Einstein was a **pacifist**, he was convinced to help develop the atomic bomb.
A **Pax** Americana will be beneficial only for America, not for other countries.

par · *equal*

    compare – *to relate, to match.*
    parallel – *corresponding, equivalent.*
    par – *a standard, a level. an average score in golf.*
    sub par – *below average, below standard, not good.*
    disparage – *to defame, to insult.*

King Street runs **parallel** with Church Street.
The team lost the championship because their performance was not up to **par**.
Mr Norman wrote a **disparaging** review of the popular movie.

path · *feeling*
pat · *suffering*
pass

    compassion – *kindness, tenderness, mercy.*
    sympathy – *understanding another's feelings, compassion.*
    antipathy – *hatred, bitterness, enmity.*
    patient – *feeling, a suffering person.*
    pathetic – *pitiful, sad, helpless.*

A doctor's **compassion** is in many ways more important than his medical knowledge.
With their bitter comments, the two rivals showed a mutual **antipathy** for each other.
The **pathetic** animals had not had any water for over a week.

patri	• father
pater	

        patricide – *killing one's father.*
        paternal – *fatherly, on the father's side of the family.*
        patriarch – *a fatherly figure, a respected old man.*

My **paternal** grandfather lived to 100 years of age.
The story of **patricide** remains one of the classic tales of all time.
Joseph Kennedy, the clan's **patriarch**, drove his children to succeed in everything.

ped   • *child*

        pediatrician – *a children's doctor.*
        pedagogue – *a forceful teacher.*
        pedophilia – *sexual attraction to children.*

If your child becomes ill, you should take her to a **pediatrician**.
Mr Morrow was a **pedagogue** and a very powerful public speaker.

ped	• foot
pod	

        pedestrian – *a person on foot, a walking person.*
        expedition – *a journey, a trip.*
        podiatrist – *a foot doctor.*
        pedal – *a lever operated by foot.*
        centipede – *an insect with many legs (100 feet).*

Cars must slow down and proceed cautiously near **pedestrian** crossings.
The hikers are planning to go on an **expedition** to the mountains this weekend.
Takashi went to see a **podiatrist** after he hurt his foot in the soccer match.

pel	• push
puls	• force

        compulsion – *a strong desire, coercion, force.*
        repel – *to force away, to disgust.*
        expel – *to drive out, to banish.*
        propel – *to drive, to throw, to force forward.*
        dispel – *to remove, to banish.*
        pulse – *a regular beating or throbbing, a heartbeat.*

Being on a diet, Al had to fight his **compulsion** to eat three large meals a day.
The spaceship is **propelled** by 4 large rockets.
The old professor tried to **dispel** rumors that he would retire soon.

pend	• hang down
pens	

        depend – *to rely on, to count on.*
        pending – *undecided, not yet formalized.*
        suspense – *anxiety, uncertainty, indecision.*
        compensate – *to balance, to repay, to counteract.*

dependent – *a person who relies on another person.*

Whether we go out today or not **depends** on the weather.
Tom's application for a patent for his invention is still **pending**.
All workers will be **compensated** for the overtime hours they put in.

---

pet   · *seek*
petit · *ask*

petition – *an application, a request signed by many people.*
appetite – *a desire, a craving.*
compete – *to play or fight against others.*

The association presented the mayor with a **petition** signed by over 5,000 people.
Those young entrepreneurs have a strong **appetite** for success.
Major established stores now have to **compete** with internet retailers.

---

petr   · *stone*
         · *rock*

petrify – *to turn into stone, to terrify.*
petroleum – *oil from the earth's crust.*
petrology – *study of rocks.*

The children were **petrified** when the raging storm shook the small cottage.
The **petroleum** industry will thrive until we find alternative sources of energy.

---

phil · *love*

philosophy – *knowledge, wisdom, (originally 'love of wisdom.')*
Philadelphia – *The City of Brotherly Love.*
philharmonic – *appreciating music, harmonious, an orchestra.*

The book compares traditional eastern and western **philosophies**.
The **Philadelphia Philharmonic** Orchestra played a new piece by Philip Glass.

---

phobia · *fear*

acrophobia – *fear of heights.*
claustrophobia – *fear of closed spaces.*
xenophobia – *fear of foreigners.*
hydrophobia – *fear of water.*

Some people who have **acrophobia** have no fear of flying.
The **claustrophobic** girl screamed when the boys locked her in the closet.
It seems that most countries and cultures have some degree of **xenophobia**.

---

phon   · *sound*
phono · *speech*

symphony – *harmony, a piece of music, a large orchestra.*
telephone – *an appliance which receives sound from far away.*
xylophone – *a musical instrument with wooden or metal bars.*
phonetics – *study of the sounds of human speech.*

Beethoven's Ninth **Symphony** is one of the most well-known pieces of music.
The invention of the **telephone** enabled people to communicate over long distances.
Language students don't need to study **phonetics** in order to learn how to speak.

photo · *light*

    photograph – *a picture made using light.*
    photophobia – *fear of light.*
    photosensitive – *sensitive to light.*
    photosynthesis – *synthesis of chemical compounds in plants.*

Her bedroom walls are covered with **photographs** and drawings of her favorite stars.
The alarm is activated by a **photosensitive** cell.
Plants obtain nutrition through the process of **photosynthesis**.

---

physic · *nature*
     · *material*

    physical – *pertaining to the body or material things.*
    physics – *the science of matter and energy.*
    physique – *the body, shape and appearance.*

The victims of the disaster suffered mental as well as **physical** trauma.
The **physics** professor couldn't explain quantum mechanics to the freshman class.
Arnold Schwarzenegger is known for his marvelous **physique**, not his acting abilities.

---

plac · *pleasant*
pleas · *favorable*

    please – *to make happy.*
    pleasant – *enjoyable, pleasing, charming.*
    placid – *calm, still, peaceful.*
    complacent – *self-satisfied, over-contented.*
    placate – *to calm, to appease someone's anger.*

The family spent a **pleasant** week camping in the mountains.
The Yankees keep winning the World Series because they don't get **complacent**.
The university president tried to **placate** the mob of angry students.

---

pli · *fold*
ple · *bend*
plex · *shape*

    pliable – *easily influenced, able to be bent.*
    pleat – *a fold in a dress, skirt, or other clothing.*
    complicated – *compound, difficult to understand.*
    complex – *having many intricate parts, intricate.*
    pliant – *flexible, soft and supple.*

The committee presented a very **complicated** plan to restructure the company.
An airplane cockpit contains a **complex** array of instruments.
The bones in a baby's body are very soft and **pliant**.

---

ple · *full*
plu

    plenty – *enough, full.*
    replenish – *to refill, to supply with more.*
    plus – *to add. additional, extra.*
    complete – *full, total. to finish.*
    complement – *to match or supplement something.*
    comply – *to obey, to agree, to conform.*

Junko **completed** the exam 30 minutes before the allotted time was up.
Red wine really **complements** this beef and mushroom dish.
All applicants must **comply** with the regulations outlined in this handbook.

polis · city

metropolis – *a large city.*
megalopolis – *a very large city encompassing several cities.*
politics – *the governmental affairs of a community.*
acropolis – *the hill in Athens.*
policy – *a plan.*

The Tokyo **Metropolitan** area has a population of over 20 million.
The Parthenon is situated on the **Acropolis**, overlooking the city of Athens.
City Council has a **policy** to attract and promote business in the downtown area.

poly · much
· many

polygamist – *a man who has many or several wives.*
polymath – *a person who is knowledgeable in many subjects.*
polytheism – *belief in many gods.*

There are still some **polygamists** in certain countries, including the United States.
It is very difficult to be a **polymath** in this era of specialization.
Polytheism is quite common in religions other than Christianity and Islam.

pon · put
posit · place

postpone – *to delay, to place after.*
position – *a place. to place.*
preposition – *a word which is placed before a noun.*
positive – *definite, unquestioned.*
component – *a part.*
juxtapose – *to put together to show contrast.*

The race has been **postponed** until the rain stops.
Beginning students often leave out **prepositions**, saying things like, "I went Boston."
A car engine is easy to understand if you break it down into its **component** parts.

popul · people
publ

popular – *known or liked by many people, famous.*
population – *the number of people living in an area.*
public – *people in general.*
publicity – *advertising, public interest.*

The **populations** of rural villages have been decreasing drastically in recent years.
The general **public** is not very interested in politics, but loves a scandal.
The rumors of the minister's affair generated lots of **publicity**.

port · carry

portable – *lightweight, able to be carried.*
transport – *to move from one place to another.*
export – *to carry out (of a country).*
import – *to carry into (a country).*

We took our **portable** stereo with us to the beach.
The company uses trains, airplanes, and trucks to **transport** its goods to retailers.
Mr Westgate made lots of money **importing** marine products into Japan.

potent · power

potent – *strong, powerful.*
impotent – *weak, powerless, afflicted with ED.*
potential – *ability.*
potentate – *a strong ruler with direct power.*

The retired politician remains one of the most **potent** figures in the party.
Ed was **impotent**, but he overcame the problem with Viagra.
Ichiro has the **potential** to play baseball in the major leagues.

press · push

pressure – *a strong force, stress.*
repress – *to hold back, to restrain.*
oppress – *to persecute, to subjugate.*
depress – *to sadden, to discourage, to push down.*
impression – *a thought, an influence, an indentation.*

Psychologists advise their patients not to **repress** their emotions.
The minority group felt as though they were being **oppressed** by the government.
My first **impression** of him was that he was not very kind, but I soon came to like him.

prim · first

primary – *the first, the most important.*
prime minister – *the leader of a government.*
primitive – *simple, crude, undeveloped.*
primeval – *prehistoric, of the first ages, ancient.*

Rick uses mostly the **primary** colors in his paintings.
We can learn about **primitive** people by studying their tools and other artifacts.
Activists are trying to stop the logging of the **primeval** forests in that country.

psych · mind

psychiatry – *treatment of mental illness.*
psychology – *the science of mental processes and behavior.*
psychopath – *a person with a personality disorder.*
psychoanalysis – *a method of analyzing mental illness.*

Psychiatry can often help people overcome their fears and insecurities.
The police believe that the woman was kidnapped by a dangerous **psychopath**.
Mr Blair overcame his depression after months of **psychoanalysis**.

put · calculate
putat · think

computation – *calculation.*
computer – *a machine originally used for calculation.*
amputate – *to cut off.*
dispute – *to argue, to think differently.*
putative – *supposed, presumed.*

The physics professor was constantly taking notes and jotting down **computations**.

The doctors **amputated** Mr Johnson's leg to prevent the cancer from spreading.
We can't **dispute** the fact that America remains the most powerful country.

Q

quer · *ask*
quisi · *seek*

inquiry – *investigation.*
requirement – *a demand, a condition.*
inquisitive – *curious.*
query – *a question.*
acquire – *to get, to obtain, to receive.*
conquer – *to overcome, to subjugate.*
prerequisite – *a necessary condition.*

We **requested** that the government carry out an **inquiry** into the alleged vote-fixing.
Sara **acquired** that house from her father after he retired and moved to Florida.
Party membership is a **prerequisite** for a career in politics.

R

rect · *right*
reg · *straight*

correct – *proper, right, exact. to improve, to edit.*
rectify – *to correct, to make proper.*
regulate – *to control, to operate properly.*
direct – *in a straight line. to lead the right way.*

Before you hand in your essay, you should **correct** all the mistakes.
The government decided to **regulate** the amount of imports.
That woman is a **direct** descendent of George Washington.

rid · *laugh*
ris

derision – *scorn, mocking laughter.*
risibility – *inclination to laughter.*
ridiculous – *laughable, funny, absurd.*

The scandal-plagued star was greeted with **derision** when he appeared.
Your decision to buy that old beat-up car was **ridiculous**.

rog · *ask*
rogat

interrogate – *to question.*
prerogative – *exclusive right or privilege.*
derogatory – *disparaging, insulting.*

Detective Stone **interrogated** the suspect for 3 hours, but didn't get much information.
I was shocked by your **derogatory** remarks.

rupt   · *break*

interrupt – *to break in.*
bankrupt – *penniless, broke, having no money left over.*
rupture – *to break. a break.*
corrupt – *evil, immoral, depraved.*

Mr Smith does not like to be **interrupted** when he is busy with his work.
When Mr Jackson's firm went **bankrupt**, he got work as a dancer at a seedy club.
Some car gasoline tanks will **rupture** in a collision and cause fires.

S

sacr   · *holy*

sacred – *holy, pure.*
sacrifice – *a holy offering. to offer or surrender something.*
sacrilege – *irreverence, blasphemy, desecration.*
consecrate – *to purify, to bless, to make completely holy.*
desecrate – *to devastate, to contaminate.*

In India, the cow is considered **sacred**.
If you want to be promoted to manager, you will have to **sacrifice** your weekends.
Vandals broke into the church at night and **desecrated** the sanctuary.

sanct   · *holy*

sanctify – *to bless, to declare holy, to give official approval.*
sanction – *to permit, to consent.   support, authorization.*
sanctity – *holiness, saintliness.*
sanctuary – *holy place, refuge, shelter.*

The newlyweds asked the priest to **sanctify** their marriage.
The army's bombing of the villages was **sanctioned** by the president.
During wartime, it seems as though people forget about the **sanctity** of human life.

scend   · *climb*

ascend – *to climb up.*
descent – *a fall, a drop, a comedown.*
transcend – *to surpass, to go beyond.*

The climbers continued to **ascend** the mountain even when snow began to fall.
The plane began its **descent** through the clouds.
The issue of the country's economic health **transcends** the question of personal taxes.

sci   · *know*
scio

science – *knowledge, technology.*
omniscient – *knowing all.*
conscious – *aware, having knowledge.*
prescient – *intuitive, having foreknowledge or foresight.*

Most people no longer believe in the existence of an **omniscient** divine being.
Man is the only animal which has been blessed with **conscious** awareness.
The novel was a **prescient** story of a president brought down by a sex scandal.

scop · watch
· view

telescope – *an instrument for viewing the stars.*
microscope – *an instrument for viewing very tiny objects.*
scope – *the range of a person's perception or thoughts.*

Astronomers used the giant **telescope** on the top of a mountain in Hawaii.
In science class, the children viewed their own blood cells through **microscopes**.
The board has decided to broaden the **scope** of the development project.

---

scrib · write
script

transcribe – *to copy, to record in writing.*
script – *writing, handwriting, a text.*
describe – *to portray, to represent.*
circumscribe – *to enclose, to limit.*
prescription – *a recipe, a written formula for medicine.*

The court clerk must **transcribe** every word that is spoken in the courtroom.
Ron has seen *Titanic* five times and read its **script** twice.
The doctor gave me a **prescription** for some powerful pain relievers.

---

sed · sit
sess · settle
sid
set

settle – *to stop, to put in place, to establish.*
session – *a meeting.*
sedentary – *inactive.*
residence – *a place where a person lives.*
sedative – *a calming or tranquilizing drug.*
sediment – *material that settles at the bottom of a liquid.*

Bob leads a **sedentary** lifestyle; he stays in, reads books, and gets little exercise.
After the children grew up and moved out, their parents moved to a smaller **residence**.
The hyperactive patient calmed down after the nurse gave him a **sedative**.

---

seg · cut
sect

section – *a separate portion or area.*
intersect – *to cut across.*
dissect – *to cut up, to analyze, to examine.*
segment – *a separate part, a component.*

We were employed by the same company, but we worked in different **sections**.
The old part of the city is **intersected** with many narrow streets.
Baby Boomers still make up the largest **segment** of society.

---

sent · think
sens · sense
· feel

sensation – *feeling.*

sensitive – *tender, emotional, showing feeling.*
consent – *to agree.*
resent – *to feel anger or indignation.*
sentiment – *feeling, opinion.*
presentiment – *a forewarning, an omen.*
sentient – *aware, knowing, thinking.*

Speed provides an exciting, though frightening, **sensation**.
The governor **consented** to meet with the protesters.
Mr Williams canceled his trip because he had a **presentiment** of disaster.

seque · *follow*
secut · *continue*
su

consecutive – *following in order.*
sequence – *an arrangement in order.*
sequel – *a continuation, a second part.*
consequence – *a result.*
persecute – *to oppress, to annoy, to bother.*
prosecute – *to accuse, to sue, to take to court.*
pursue – *to chase.*

The Lions won seven **consecutive** playoff games before losing in the final.
The movie *Titanic* was a huge success, but it's doubtful if there will be a **sequel**.
The attorney decided to **prosecute** after the police found new, convincing evidence.

serv · *serve*
· *keep*

conserve – *to save, to avoid wasting something.*
deserve – *to merit, to earn.*
reserve – *to keep, to promise.*
preserve – *to maintain in the same state.*
servile – *submissive, obsequious.*
subservient – *subordinate, obedient, ingratiating.*

The government launched a campaign to get people to **conserve** energy.
Ms Hall's sales program has been a failure, so she doesn't **deserve** a raise this year.
The U.N. forces were unable to **preserve** the peace in that country.

sinu · *fold*
· *bend*

sinuate – *winding, curvy.*
insinuate – *to hint, to suggest.*
sinuous – *crooked, meandering.*

The magazine report **insinuated** that the president was involved in the scandal.
We drove carefully along the **sinuous** mountain road.

soci · *companion*

sociable – *friendly, gregarious, amiable.*
associate – *to accompany, to collaborate.*
dissociate – *to separate, to disconnect.*

Sociable children often do better in school than quiet children.

Sociable children often do better in school than quiet children.
Mr Last is a ruthless businessman who has been known to **associate** with the Mafia.
Al Gore tried to **dissociate** himself from President Clinton after the scandal.

sol · *one*

solitary – *alone, deserted.*
solitude – *isolation, detachment.*
solo – *alone. music performed by one person.*
soliloquy – *a speech by one person in a play.*
desolate – *lonely, deserted, barren.*

Few people noticed the quiet, **solitary** man sitting at the end of the bar.
Most people are familiar with the first lines of Hamlet's **soliloquy**.
We drove for hours through the **desolate** landscape of Death Valley.

solv · *loosen*
solut

dissolve – *to melt, to separate, to finish.*
absolve – *to excuse, to free from blame.*
absolute – *complete.*

This powder will **dissolve** instantly when you pour hot water on it.
The falsely-accused man was soon **absolved** of any involvement in the robbery.
President Amin was a strong leader who held **absolute** power.

somn · *sleep*

somnambulist – *a sleep walker.*
insomnia – *the inability to sleep.*
somnolent – *sleepy.*

I thought I saw a ghost, but soon realized my new roommate was a **somnambulist**.
The doctor gave me some potent sleeping pills to combat my **insomnia**.

son · *sound*

unison – *harmony, singing together in similar voices.*
sonorous – *having a full, rich sound.*
sonic boom – *the explosive sound of a jet flying overhead.*
dissonance – *harsh or inharmonious sound, discordant sound.*

The people all shouted in **unison** when the president came out of his plane.
The bells in the large clock in the town square rang out each hour **sonorously**.
Concert-goers were shocked by the **dissonance** of the composer's strange new work.

sophi · *wise*

sophisticated – *wise, worldly, refined, complex.*
philosopher – *a thinker, a lover of wisdom.*
theosophy – *doctrine of the knowledge of God.*

Sharon became quite **sophisticated** after she left her hometown and moved to the city.
Like most **philosophers,** Nietzsche is misunderstood by the masses.
Theosophists claim to have received divine revelations and to have mystical insights.

soror · *sister*

sorority – *a college club or dorm for women.*
sororicide – *killing one's sister.*
Erika was admitted to one of the elite **sororities** at her university.
The story was a morbid tale of **sororicide** and other hideous crimes.

spect • *look*

spectator – *an observer.*
aspect – *an appearance.*
circumspect – *cautious, careful, looking around.*
inspect – *to examine, to study closely.*
perspective – *viewpoint, outlook, insight.*

Over 50,000 **spectators** can be seated in that stadium.
Try to be more **circumspect** when dealing with people you don't know very well.
From a historical **perspective**, it seems as if the problem will not be resolved soon.

spir • *breath*
       • *spirit*

respiration – *breathing.*
inspire – *to stimulate, to animate, to affect.*
perspire – *to sweat.*
spirit – *an angel, the mind or soul.*

The patient grew weaker and weaker as his **respiration** grew fainter.
Our coach **inspired** us to play harder and to fight till the end.
The human **spirit** can remain strong in the face of extreme difficulty.

stab • *stand*
stat
stant

establish – *to begin, to set up.*
stable – *solid, standing firmly, unchanging.*
statue – *a standing sculpture.*
distant – *standing apart.*
circumstance – *condition, situation, occasion.*
station – *a location, a stop. to place, to position.*

Bill Gates dropped out of Harvard to **establish** Microsoft.
After the accident, the injured driver was in serious but **stable** condition.
Police were investigating the **circumstances** surrounding the kidnapping.

sting   • *prick*
stinct • *mark*

distinct – *separate, clear, well-defined.*
instinct – *natural knowledge.*
extinct – *non-existent, vanished, obsolete.*
extinguish – *to put out, to suppress, to finish.*

The history of that country can be divided into two **distinct** periods.
Dogs have a natural **instinct** to hunt, and training will help them to use this **instinct**.
Firefighters managed to **extinguish** the blaze before it spread to other buildings.

strain • *tie*

string
    constraint – *pressure, force, stress, repression.*
    restrict – *to hold back, to confine.*
    strenuous – *exhausting, laborious.*
    strict – *severe, rigid.*
    astringent – *rigid, simple, austere.*

They couldn't buy that large house due to financial **constraints**.
My father tried to avoid **strenuous** exercise after his operation.
Mr Pemberton is a **strict** teacher who demands complete obedience in his class.

---

stru   • *build*
stro
    construct – *to build, to erect.*
    obstruction – *an obstacle, a blockade, a barricade.*
    destroy – *to ruin, to demolish.*
    instrument – *a tool used to make things.*

Many companies worked together to **construct** that large building.
The streets of the city were filled with **obstructions** after the riots.
Large parts of the city were **destroyed** by bombs during the war.

---

surg   • *rise*
surrect
    surge – *a large increase, a rise, a flood.*
    insurgent – *rebellious. a rebel, a traitor.*
    resurrect – *to bring back to life.*

There was a **surge** of imports after the government lowered import duties.
The army put down the rebellion by the **insurgents** and arrested their leaders.
After overcoming his addiction to drugs, John **resurrected** his career as a musician.

T

tang   • *touch*
ting
tact
tain
    contact – *to meet, to get in touch with.*
    tangible – *real, noticeable, substantial, able to be touched.*
    attach – *to add, to affix, to stick to.*
    contingent – *dependent, incidental.*
    attain – *to get, to accomplish, to reach.*
    abstain – *to avoid, to refrain from using.*

The increase in car sales is **tangible** evidence that the economy is improving.
You will never **attain** your goals if you are not prepared to work hard.
Mr Watts has **abstained** from alcohol for over one year now.

---

tect   • *artistry*
tech   • *skill*

text – *written material, a composition.*
architect – *a person who designs buildings.*
technique – *the method or study of an art or process.*
technology – *the application of science to industry.*

The professor lost the **text** of his speech, so he made his presentation from memory.
The guitarist is not very talented, but he has a good grasp of **technique**.
Information **technology** has changed the way we work and communicate.

tele · *distant*
· *far*

television – *an appliance which receives scenes from far away.*
telescope – *an instrument for seeing things far away.*
telegram – *a written message from far away.*

The astronomers plan to study the comet through the university's **telescope**.
Telegrams were very useful before the rise of the Internet.

tempor · *time*

contemporary – *of the same time, modern, recent.*
extemporaneous – *spontaneous, impromptu.*
temporary – *for a short time.*

Pop music is only one type of **contemporary** music.
The young student got onto the platform and made an **extemporaneous** speech.
I'm going to look for a **temporary** job to make some cash before school starts.

ten · *hold*
tain

contain – *to hold within.*
obtain – *to get, to acquire.*
tenure – *holding office, occupancy.*
tenacious – *strong, holding strongly.*

Anyone wishing to take time off will have to **obtain** permission from the director.
The Soviet Union disintegrated during Gorbachev's **tenure**.
The victim was unable to escape from the **tenacious** grasp of his attacker.

tend · *stretch*
tin · *extend*

continue – *to keep on, to last.*
contend – *to present an argument, to fight against.*
intensify – *to become stronger, to sharpen.*
superintendent – *a director, someone in charge.*

The leader **contended** that his party would be able to keep the economy strong.
Competition in the industry **intensified** when the large company went bankrupt.
The **superintendent** of the building is responsible for repairs and upkeep.

tenu · *narrow*
· *thin*

tenuous – *weak, insubstantial.*
attenuate – *to weaken, to reduce, to thin out.*

tenuous – *weak, insubstantial.*
extenuating – *making less serious, partly excusing.*

The leaders put off the election because their position was very **tenuous**.
The policeman let the speeder go because there were **extenuating** circumstances.

---

term   • *end*
termin

terminal – *last, permanent, incurable.*
terminus – *the last stop of a bus or train.*
term – *a limited period of time.*
exterminate – *to destroy completely, to annihilate.*

The doctor determined that Paul has **terminal** cancer.
According to this travel guide, Beijing is the eastern **terminus** of the Orient Express.
The American Indians were almost **exterminated** by European settlers.

---

terr   • *land*
            • *earth*

terrestrial – *pertaining to the earth.*
subterranean – *underground.*
extraterrestrial – *not from this earth, alien, ET.*
territory – *an area of land, a region.*

The new biology course focuses on both **terrestrial** and aquatic animals.
Some architects have been trying to develop and promote **subterranean** housing.
The polar regions and many mountain ranges still contain much unexplored **territory**.

---

test   • *witness*

protest – *to object, to complain.*
testimony – *evidence, a declaration of truth.*
testify – *to bear witness to declare.*
detest – *to hate, to abhor.*

We are planning a huge rally to **protest** the government's scandalous behavior.
The jury had to take into account the **testimony** of the three eyewitnesses.
The third eyewitness **testified** that she had seen the accused running from the scene.

---

theo   • *god*

atheist – *a person who doesn't believe in god.*
pantheon – *a group of gods, a group of god-like figures.*
theology – *study of god.*

Although Stan was raised in a Jewish family, he is now an **atheist**.
The Beatles and the Rolling Stones remain at the pinnacle of the rock music **pantheon**.
Theology is not limited to the study of any single religion.

---

therm   • *heat*

thermometer – *an instrument to measure heat.*
thermostat – *an instrument to control temperature.*
thermodynamics – *science of the relation of heat and energy.*

It looks like a sunny and warm day, but the **thermometer** reads minus 2.
During the energy crisis, most people set their house **thermostats** at 68 degrees F.

tort · *twist*
tors

  distort – *to deform, to mutilate, to disfigure, to change.*
  contort – *to twist out of shape.*
  torsion – *twisting or turning, stress resulting from twisting.*
  torture – *to punish with severe pain. intense suffering.*

The controversial author accused the media of **distorting** his views.
Contorted figures were a common sight on the stage of the modern dance festival.
Many prisoners of war were **tortured** and killed by the rebel army.

tract · *pull*
  · *attract*

  attract – *to lure, to draw towards.*
  extract – *to take out.*
  subtract – *to take away from.*
  retract – *to take back.*

Disneyland **attracts** people of all ages.
A huge oil field was found under the sea, but engineers may not be able to **extract** it.
The mayor was forced to **retract** his statement about the city's resident foreigners.

U

urb · *city*

  urban – *pertaining to a city.*
  urbane – *sophisticated, elegant, cultured.*
  suburb – *an area outside a city center.*
  exurb – *a residential area outside a city.*

Urban sprawl has changed the character of cities throughout the world.
Anyone who meets Colin will be impressed by his **urbane** and charming manner.
Many people prefer to live in the **suburbs** after starting a family.

V

vac · *empty*

  vacuum – *a void, an empty space.*
  vacant – *empty, unoccupied.*
  evacuate – *to leave, to evict, to escape.*
  vacation – *a holiday, free time.*

The death of the president left a power **vacuum** which lasted for over a month.
Homeless people often gather in that **vacant** lot on King Street.
Residents were told to **evacuate** the area after the accident at the nuclear plant.

val · *valuable*
vail · *strong*

  evaluate – *to determine the value, to make a judgment.*
  equivalent – *of equal value, having the same qualities.*
  prevalent – *predominant, popular, common.*

valor – *courage.*

All teachers must fairly **evaluate** the performance of each of their students.
A computer in that poor country costs the **equivalent** of three month's salary.
Smoking became **prevalent** in developing countries with the increase in advertising.

---

ven · *come*
vent

  intervene – *to mediate, to interfere, to arbitrate.*
  prevent – *to stop, to suppress, to prohibit.*
  convention – *a meeting, an assembly.*

Referees will not **intervene** in a fight between hockey players unless it's safe to do so.
The annual **convention** of Mac users attracts people from throughout the world.
Veni, vidi, vici. (Latin for "I came, I saw, I conquered.")

---

ver · *true*

  very – *truly.*
  verify – *to prove the truth of something.*
  verdict – *a judgment, a statement that something is true.*

The police were able to **verify** the suspect's alibi.
The jury is expected to pass a **verdict** of 'not guilty.'
In vino veritas. (Latin for "There is truth in wine.")

---

verb · *word*

  verbalize – *to express in words.*
  verbose – *wordy, talkative.*
  verbatim – *word-for-word, literal.*

Their relationship improved after they learned how to **verbalize** their feelings.
Voters are sick and tired of hearing **verbose** politicians on TV every night.
The professor's comments were reported **verbatim** in the school newspaper.

---

vert · *turn*
vers · *change*

  convert – *to change, to transform.*
  divert – *to turn aside, to interrupt, to amuse.*
  versatile – *adaptable, having many skills.*
  inverted – *reversed, turned around.*
  revert – *to change back, to reverse.*

The government is encouraging homeowners to **convert** to solar heating systems.
Rob is a great actor in comedy roles, but he's not very **versatile**.
Many elderly immigrants **revert** to using their first language as they grow older.

---

via · *way*
voy
vey

  deviation – *departure from the correct way.*
  viaduct – *a bridge.*
  obvious – *clear, plain.*
  voyage – *a trip.*

convey – *to transfer, to express.*

The director will not tolerate any **deviation** from the script by the actors.
The **obvious** choice was for us to turn back, since the road was completely washed out.
The **viaduct** was built after the war to connect the two sides of the growing city.

v i d • *see*
v i s

    vision – *sight.*
    evidence – *proof, things seen.*
    vista – *view, scene, landscape.*
    visual – *optical, pertaining to sight.*

There was no **evidence** that the suspect had been at the scene of the crime.
From our cabin window, we saw a wonderful **vista** of snow-covered mountains.
That school is for the blind and other **visually** handicapped people.

v i n c • *conquer*
v i c
vanqu

    victory – *triumph, win, conquest.*
    invincible – *unbeatable, powerful, unconquerable.*
    vanquish – *to defeat, to overpower.*
    convince – *to persuade, to win over.*

The team celebrated its championship **victory** with a few bottles of champagne.
Until they were beaten in the playoffs, it seemed as if The Giants were **invincible**.
The salesman **convinced** the customer to buy the more expensive car.

v i v • *life*
v i t

    vivid – *brilliant, distinct.*
    vital – *necessary, important, alive, active.*
    revive – *to recover, to come back to life.*
    survive – *to remain alive.*
    vivacious – *animated, energetic.*

I've been having some **vivid** dreams recently.
Interest in The Beatles has been **revived** with the release of yet another anthology.
Mihoko brightened up the party with her **vivacious** personality and hearty laugh.
"Ars longa, vita brevis." (Latin for "Art is long, life is short.")

v o c • *call*
v o k • *speak*

    provoke – *to annoy, to stimulate, to make angry.*
    revoke – *to recall, to cancel, to repeal.*
    evoke – *to call out, to elicit, to inspire.*
    invoke – *to plead, to summon, to refer to a principle.*
    invocation – *a plea, a calling to prayer.*
    advocate – *to support, to promote. a supporter.*

Although the kids did nothing to **provoke** their father, he became very angry.
Ted had his driver's license **revoked** after he was caught driving while drunk.

Ted had his driver's license **revoked** after he was caught driving while drunk.
Many people voted for George W. Bush only because he **advocated** a large tax cut.

---

vol · will
· wish

volunteer – *a person who does work for no pay.*
voluntarily – *freely, intentionally, of one's own will.*
volition – *will, ambition, discipline.*
involuntary – *not planned, not intended, not controllable.*

They **volunteer** as part-time gardeners and do other **voluntary** activities at the park.
The murder suspect went to the police of his own **volition** and confessed to the crime.
Mr Moore has had an **involuntary** twitch in his neck since his nervous breakdown.

---

volv · roll
volu

revolve – *to turn, to circle, to rotate.*
evolve – *to develop, to transform, to roll out.*
convoluted – *confusing, coiled, twisted, intricate.*
involve – *to include, to associate, to concern.*
evolution – *development, the history of the earth.*

The moon **revolves** around the earth once every 28 days.
Even though that long book has a **convoluted** plot, most people find it easy to read.
The job of teaching **involves** 3-4 hours of preparation for each hour of class.

PREFIXES

a—

a—	• (verb prefix)

awaken – *to wake up, to wake a person up.*
amuse – *to entertain.*
assure – *to guarantee, to convince.*
appoint – *to designate for a position, to set.*

While camping, we were **awakened** each morning by the sound of birds.
They kept lots of toys in their house to **amuse** their visiting grandchildren.
The teacher **appointed** Madoka and Minori to be the leaders of the debate teams.

a—	• toward
	• at

aloud – *not silently.*
akin – *similar, alike, related to.*
away – *not present.*
aground – *to the ground.*

I read these stories **aloud** to my children at bedtime.
Football and hockey are rough sports, more **akin** to war than to other sports.
The boat ran **aground** while the drunk captain was trying to navigate through the fog.

a b—	• from
a b s—	• away

absent – *to be away, not present.*
abduct – *to kidnap.*
abscond – *to take away.*
abject – *shameful, depressing, lowly.*

If you are **absent** from a class, you must pick up your material within the next week.
In the slums of Brazil's major cities, we saw people living in **abject** poverty.
We thought we could trust our partner, but he **absconded** with the funds.

a—	• not
a n—	• without

apolitical – *uninterested in politics.*
anonymous – *nameless, unknown, unnamed.*
asymmetrical – *uneven, having two different sides.*
asexual – *sexless.*
anarchy – *lack of government, chaos.*
anemic – *pale, weak due to lack of blood.*
anesthetize – *to deprive of feeling.*

The newspaper received an **anonymous** letter warning them not to publish the story.
The government collapsed and the country plunged into a state of **anarchy**.
The nurse **anesthetized** the patient before the operation.

ad–	• to
ac–	• forward
af–	
ag–	
al–	
an–	
ap–	
ar–	
as–	
at–	

adhere – *to stick, to be devoted.*
adapt – *to change, to conform.*
adverb – *a word which modifies a verb.*
acknowledge – *to admit, to recognize.*
acquiesce – *to submit, to comply.*
affix – *to attach something.*
aggregate – *total, sum. grouped together.*
allure – *to attract, to tempt.*
annex – *to take, to attach. an addition.*
approach – *to come near.*
arrange – *to put in order.*
associate – *to deal with, to relate, to unite.*
attend – *to accompany, to serve, to visit.*

Suzzee was suspended from school because she did not **adhere** to the dress code.
Miles Davis is **acknowledged** as a master of jazz.
Simon's parents warned him not to **associate** with bad kids like Harry and Ron.

ambi–	• both
amphi–	

ambidextrous – *skilled with both hands.*
ambiguous – *having two meanings, unclear, confusing.*
ambivalent – *possessing conflicting emotions.*
amphibious – *able to live both on land and in water.*

The diplomat called a press conference to clarify yesterday's **ambiguous** statements.
Lisa proved her love for Tom, but he remained **ambivalent** about their relationship.
The army used **amphibious** vehicles when it attacked the coastal city.

ante–	• before

antecedent – *a preceding event or word.*
antechamber – *a front room.*
antedate – *to come before.*
ante meridiem – *morning, a.m. (e.g., 10:00 a.m.)*

Study of the historical **antecedents** will help you understand the current situation.
His office is an **antechamber** to the C.E.O.'s suite of offices.
Although 12:00 ***a.m.*** denotes noon, it is better to say *12:00 noon*, to avoid confusion.

anti– • opposed to
 • against
  antipathy – *hatred, hostility.*
  anti-social – *unfriendly, cynical, misanthropic.*
  antithesis – *an opposite view, a contrasting movement.*
  anti-nuclear – *against nuclear power.*

His strong statements clearly showed his **antipathy** to such outrageous behavior.
Some people say that excessive computer use leads to **anti-social** behavior.
The **anti-nuclear** rally attracted thousands of demonstrators opposed to the new plant.

---

apo– • *from*
 • *reverse*
 • *off*
  apology – *a speech in defense of something, an explanation.*
  apotheosis – *deification, exaltation to divine rank, an ideal.*
  apogee – *the farthest point of an orbit, the highest point.*
  apocalypse – *a revelation, a prophecy.*

The manager sent us a letter of **apology** concerning the waitress's rude behavior.
That ancient culture had reached its **apogee** by about 1500 B.C.
Every few years, another fringe group appears, warning of an impending **apocalypse**.

---

arch– • *first*
 • *chief*
  archetype – *an original model, an excellent example.*
  archbishop – *a chief bishop.*
  archaeology – *study of first things or ancient things.*
  archenemy – *one's worst enemy.*

Hanh is the **archetype** of the highly motivated and over-achieving Asian student.
The **archaeologist** was accused of faking the findings of important historical artifacts.
Those two defensemen were **archenemies** before they became linemates after a trade.

---

auto– • *self*
  autobiography – *the story of a person's life written by himself.*
  automobile – *a vehicle that moves itself.*
  autocracy – *rule by a single person, dictatorship.*

Few people were surprised when Kurt Cobain's **autobiography** turned out to be fake.
While Asians use public transportation, Americans rely primarily on the **automobile**.
Even many undeveloped countries are moving away from **autocracy**.

---

b—

be– • *do* (verb prefix)
 • *make*
  belittle – *to degrade, to insult, to disparage.*
  befriend – *to make someone a friend.*
  bestir – *to make active.*
  besmirch – *to make dirty, to dishonor, to tarnish.*

We tried hard to please our boss, but he always responded by **belittling** our efforts.

Erin knew no-one when she first moved here, but her classmates soon **befriended** her.
The lawyers managed to **besmirch** the reputation of the defendant before the trial.

c—

cata– · against
· down

catastrophe – *a disaster.*
catalyst – *an agent, something which causes an action.*
catapult – *to throw quickly, suddenly, and forcefully.*

The oil spill was an environmental **catastrophe** for those beautiful islands.
The recession was a **catalyst** for changes in the country's economic and social policy.
Graeme jumped up in a rage and **catapulted** the table across the room.

co–   · together
com– · with
con–
col–
cor–

copilot – *one of a pair of pilots.*
cooperate – *to agree with, to work together in harmony.*
coexist – *to live side-by-side.*
compatriot – *a fellow countryman.*
colleague – *a fellow worker, a co-worker.*
correlation – *a connection, a similarity, a relationship.*
collapse – *to fall down, to cave in.*
communicate – *to correspond with others.*

The **coalition** government will **collapse** if the two parties don't **cooperate**.
I love working for this great company, but sometimes my **colleagues** get on my nerves.
There is a very clear **correlation** between smoking and lung cancer.

contra–   · against
contro–   · opposing
counter–

contradict – *to disagree, to challenge, to say the opposite.*
controversy – *a dispute, an argument.*
contrary – *conflicting, opposite.*
counteract – *to neutralize, to oppose, to offset.*
counterproductive – *not productive, not effective.*

The police report **contradicted** the version given by most of the eyewitnesses.
The government's strong-arm tactics have incited lots of **controversy**.
My doctor told me not to drink coffee, since it will **counteract** the effects of the drugs.

d—

d e—
- *down*
- *away*

debase – *to defile, to belittle, to lower in value.*
depart – *to leave, to go away.*
decadent – *immoral, depraved, degenerate.*
descend – *to go down.*
detract – *to obstruct, to take away from.*

The plane is scheduled to **depart** at 6:45 p.m.
Most people were shocked by the revelations of the rock star's **decadent** lifestyle.
Everyone turned to look as the model gracefully **descended** the stairs.

d i a—
- *across*
- *through*

diagonal – *a slanting line.*
diameter – *a line passing through the center of a circle.*
diagram – *an outline drawing.*

The **diagonal** rays of the sun fell on the coffee table in the center of the room.
The 2-meter **diameter** steel pipe fell off the truck and rolled across the parking lot.
We added charts and **diagrams** to the report to make it easier to understand.

d i s—
d i f—
d i—
- *not*
- *opposite*
- *away*

disinterested – *not involved, not interested.*
differ – *to disagree.*
disappear – *to vanish, to fade away.*
disagreeable – *unpleasant, undesirable, unhelpful.*
dishonest – *not honest, untruthful.*
digress – *to meander, to turn away.*

His friends joined in the riot, but Rick remained a **disinterested** observer.
The plane veered off to the north and **disappeared** into the clouds.
Shinichi may be a skillful businessman, but he still has a **disagreeable** personality.

d y s—
- *faulty*
- *difficult*

dysfunctional – *not functioning well, not normal.*
dyslexia – *difficulty in reading properly.*
dystrophy – *defective nutrition.*

Sean lacks social skills because he grew up in a **dysfunctional** family.
Barry was quite smart, but he didn't do well in school due to his **dyslexia**.
Muscular **dystrophy** is a terrible disease in which one's muscles slowly deteriorate.

e—

en– · *make*
em– · *(verb prefix)*
  enlighten – *to inform, to educate.*
  endanger – *to cause danger.*
  embody – *to personify, to be a symbol, to contain.*
  empower – *to make strong, to give power.*

Professor Usami **enlightened** us with regard to the proper forms of the conditional.
The recent bombings have **endangered** the peace talks between the two sides.
The young charismatic leader **embodied** the hopes of his generation.

epi– · *on*
  · *after*
  · *over*
  epitome – *the best example, an ideal representative.*
  epilogue – *a concluding part of a book.*
  epitaph – *words written on a tombstone.*
  epicenter – *the spot above the center of an earthquake.*
  epidermis – *the outer layer of skin.*

The Macintosh is the **epitome** of the user-friendly computer.
His **epitaph** simply said, "He was never here, and now he's gone."
The **epicenter** of the earthquake was 20 kilometers southwest of the downtown area.

eu– · *good*
u–
  euphemism – *a pleasant word (substituted for a blunt word).*
  utopia – *a perfect world, a good society.*
  eulogy – *a speech honoring a person who has died.*
  euphoria – *a feeling of great happiness or well-being.*

Instead of saying "lay off workers," Ford used the **euphemism** "restructure."
John was called "a hero" in the **eulogy** given by his friend at the funeral.
There was **euphoria** throughout the nation after the end of the war was announced.

ex– · *out*
e – · *from*
  expel – *to drive out.*
  extreme – *outermost, excessive.*
  express – *to say something, to state, to communicate.*
  exclude – *to shut out, to restrict.*
  expatriate – *a person living outside his native country.*
  emit – *to send out, to discharge, to radiate.*
  evolve – *to develop, to come out.*

Suzzee was **expelled** from school because she refused to adhere to the dress code.
For many years, women were **excluded** from that school.
The growing number of **expatriates** is having a profound effect on Japanese society.

ex– • *former*

    ex-husband – *a former husband.*
    ex-president – *a former president.*
    ex-girlfriend – *a former girlfriend.*

She got lots of money from her **ex-husband** after the divorce.
Like most men, Mike was terribly afraid of running into his **ex-girlfriend** again.

extra– • *beyond*
       • *outside*

    extraordinary – *exceptional.*
    extra-curricular – *outside the items in a curriculum.*
    extra territorial – *beyond the borders of a nation.*
    extraterrestrial – *not of this earth, an alien, ET.*

Hiroko has made **extraordinary** progress in English in the past year.
Not only did he do well in his studies, he was also active in **extra-curricular** activities.
Those crazy scientists have been studying **extraterrestrial** rocks for signs of life.

f—

fore– • *front*
      • *previous*

    forecast – *to predict, to estimate. a prediction.*
    foreleg – *the front leg of an animal.*
    forethought – *planning, preparation, caution.*

The weather **forecast** said it would snow today.
The horse suffered a slight fracture of its **foreleg**, so it was shot.
You could have prevented the accident with a little **forethought**.

h—

hemi– • *half*

    hemisphere – *half of a ball, half of the earth.*
    hemihydrate – *a mixture of half water and half other molecules.*
    hemicycle – *half of a circle.*

Some stars can be seen from only the northern **hemisphere**.

hetero– • *different*
        • *other*

    heterosexual – *attracted to the opposite sex.*
    heterodoxy – *unorthodox, having different beliefs.*
    heterogeneous – *different, consisting of dissimilar parts.*

Although Debby is a lesbian, she has many **heterosexual** friends.
Some people can't appreciate the **heterogeneous** societies of cities such as New York.

homo– • *same*
    homosexual – *attracted to the same sex.*
    homonyms – *words with the same sound and spelling.*
    homogeneous – *having the same characteristics, pure.*

Some liberal governments now allow marriage of **homosexuals**.
The natives of those Pacific islands are all part of an ethnically **homogeneous** group.

---

i–

---

in–	• *in*
en–	• *upon*
em–	• *toward*

    install – *to put in.*
    include – *to contain, to hold.*
    incision – *a surgical cut.*
    empathy – *kindness, compassion.*
    enclose – *to shut in.*

The Fire Department insisted that we **install** sprinklers in the building.
The surgeon made a small **incision** in the patient's neck.
I have **enclosed** $15.00 in this envelope as payment for the book you sent.

in–	• *not*
il–	• *without*
im–	
ir–	

    inconsequential – *not important.*
    insatiable – *not able to be satisfied.*
    intestate – *without a last will and testament.*
    illegal – *unlawful, prohibited.*
    immature – *young, not developed.*
    immoral – *corrupt, evil, lacking morals.*
    improper – *not right.*
    irregular – *not regular, without a pattern.*

Please don't drag the meeting on too long by discussing **inconsequential** details.
Dorothy has an **insatiable** appetite for sweets.
She was a very sensible woman, but actually quite **immature** emotionally.

---

inter– • *between*

    intervene – *to mediate, to interfere, to arbitrate.*
    interject – *to interrupt.*
    international – *between nations.*
    intermission – *a short break between two sessions.*

The referee **intervened** when the two players started fighting.
The moderator let the two candidates debate for minutes at a time, rarely **interjecting**.
Since tonight's movie is 3 hours long, there will be a short **intermission** at 8:30.

intra– • *within*
intro–

intrastate – *within a state.*
intramural – *within the bounds of a school or institution.*
introspective – *contemplative, having private thoughts.*

Our team made it to the **intrastate** championships, but didn't get to the nationals.
All students have the chance to participate in **intramural** sports.
She is a quiet, **introspective** person who spends hours alone in her room.

m—

macro– • *huge*
• *large*

macroclimate – *the climate of a large area.*
macrocosm – *the entire universe, a large world.*
macroevolution – *evolution involving entire species.*
macroeconomics – *study of overall aspects of an economy.*

The **macroclimate** of that country can be described as dry and warm.
The microcosm of a living organism is as expansive as the **macrocosm** of the universe.
The new governor's focus on **macroeconomics** came under attack.

magna– • *large*
magni– • *great*

magnify – *to make larger.*
magnificent – *wonderful, awesome.*
magnitude – *greatness of size or rank.*
magnanimous – *big-hearted, great-spirited.*

We could make out the details only after we **magnified** the picture 500%.
I didn't realize the **magnitude** of the problem until it was almost too late.
The losing candidate **magnanimously** congratulated the new president-elect.

mal– • *bad*
• *wrong*

malevolent – *evil, bad-willed.*
malefactor – *an evil-doer.*
malnutrition – *lack of proper foods or nutrition.*

He was a **malevolent** politician who hurt everyone he dealt with.
The skilled lawyer helped many **malefactors** stay out of prison.
The leaders of North Korea live in luxury, while the people suffer from **malnutrition**.

meg– • *big*
max– • *great*
maj–

megabyte – *1 million bytes of data (in a computer).*
maximum – *the greatest amount, the best.*
majority – *the most, the maximum, the largest number.*

New computers have over 80 **megabytes** of RAM.

The **maximum** speed limit on this road is 120 kilometers per hour.
The **majority** of students live on campus, while only a few live in town.

---

micro– • very small
 • tiny

  microbe – bacteria, a germ.
  microscope – an instrument for viewing very tiny objects.
  microwave – a short electric wave, an oven.
  microcosm – a small model of the world, a small world.
  Microsoft – a small-minded company.

You will be able to see those **microbes** only through a **microscope**.
Microwaves are quick and convenient, but the jury's still out regarding their safety.

---

mini– • small

  diminish – to become smaller, to lessen.
  minimize – to reduce, to lessen.
  minimum – the least, the smallest amount.
  miniature – tiny, a small model.

The influence of the party chairman has **diminished** in the last few years.
You can **minimize** the risk of disease by eating a healthy, well-balanced diet.
The labor unions were pleased when the **minimum** wage was increased to $10.00.

---

mis– • wrong

  misunderstand – to confuse, to interpret wrongly.
  mistrust – to doubt, to suspect. suspicion.
  misplace – to lose.
  misbehave – to act improperly, to disobey.

It seems as if many people **misunderstood** what the book was trying to say.
There is a growing **mistrust** of elected officials.
I've **misplaced** my keys again. Can you help me find them?

---

mis– • hate
miso–

  misanthropy – hatred of mankind.
  misogynist – a hater of women.
  misoneism – hatred of new things, hatred of change.
  miso soup – hateful Japanese fermented bean soup.

His grandfather was a **misanthropic** person who nevertheless succeeded in business.
That charming actor had affairs with many women, but at heart he was a **misogynist**.

---

multi– • many
 • much

  multiply – to become many, to make many.
  multifaceted – many-sided, complex.
  multitude – a huge crowd of people, a large number of things.
  multilingual – able to speak several languages very well.

Dave is a **multifaceted** artist; he writes, paints, acts, and makes music.
The Pope was met by **multitudes** of people wherever he went.
Mr Riley claims to be **multilingual**, but he can speak only two languages very well.

n—

neo— · *new*

    neologism – *a new word.*
    neoclassicism – *a revival of classical ideas.*
    neo-Nazi – *a present-day Nazi.*

The IT revolution has spawned such **neologisms** as 'cyberspace' and 'e-commerce.'
Many of America's government buildings were constructed in the **neoclassical** style.
German police have arrested several **neo-Nazis** in connection with the arson attack.

non— · *not*

    nonviolent – *peaceful.*
    nonconformist – *a rebel, a free thinker, a maverick.*
    nonsense – *foolishness. foolish, silly.*
    nonentity – *a nobody, an insignificant person.*

Although he looks and acts like an ordinary citizen, he's actually a **non-conformist**.
The doctor dismissed her claim to be terribly sick as complete **nonsense**.
After losing the election, the unsuccessful candidate was seen as a political **nonentity**.

o—

ob— · *to*
oc— · *toward*
of— · *against*
op—

    obsequious – *obedient, submissive, servile.*
    obtain – *to get, to acquire.*
    occur – *to happen.*
    offer – *to give, to present.*
    oppose – *to resist, to be against.*

Tim's boss and colleagues were appalled by his **obsequious** behavior.
All applicant's must **obtain** a certificate of health from the company doctor.
Most consumers strongly **oppose** the prime minister's plan to raise the sales tax.

omni— · *all*

    omniscient – *all-knowing.*
    omnipotent – *all-powerful.*
    omnivorous – *eating both meats and vegetables.*
    omnipresent – *everywhere, present in all places at one time.*

Students may think that teachers are **omniscient**, but teachers know better than that.
Such **omnivorous** animals will eat anything they can find.
Even after living in the city for years, I can't get used to the **omnipresent** traffic noise.

over– • *too much*

    oversleep – *to sleep too late.*
    overpopulation – *too many people living in an area.*
    overpowering – *strong, irresistible.*

I'm sorry I'm late. I **overslept**.
Overpopulation has become a severe problem in many of the world's largest cities.
I've tried to quit smoking, but I always get an **overpowering** urge to light up again.

p—

para– • *beside*
     • *beyond*

    paramount – *most important.*
    parapsychology – *psychology dealing with the abnormal.*
    paraphrase – *to rewrite a text in a different form.*

For parents, the welfare of their children should be of **paramount** importance.
The well-known doctor was criticized for his interest in **parapsychology**.
The difficult science book was **paraphrased** to make it easier to understand.

per– • *through*
     • *completely*
     • *around*

    permit – *to let through, to allow entrance.*
    percolate – *to drip through.*
    periphery – *an edge, a surrounding area.*
    perimeter – *the outer boundary.*
    perennial – *long-lasting, endless, throughout the year.*

She served us freshly **percolated** coffee and hot cinnamon buns.
They built a log cabin on the **periphery** of the national park.
Until Vantage published *Vocab-ability*, there had been a **perennial** shortage of useful vocabulary reference books.

poly– • *many*
     • *much*

    polytheism – *belief in many gods.*
    polygamy – *marriage to several spouses at the same time.*
    polyglot – *a person who speaks many languages.*
    polygon – *a many-sided figure.*

Polygamy is banned in all developed societies.
My French teacher is a **polyglot** who speaks and reads four languages.

post– • *after*

    posterity – *future generations, descendants.*
    posthumous – *after death.*
    post-mortem – *a medical examination of a dead body.*
    post meridiem – *afternoon, p.m. (e.g. 10:00 p.m.)*

A monument to the country's first leader was erected for **posterity**.
The late poet became famous after the **posthumous** publication of her book.

The city coroner carried out a **post-mortem** on the body of the young man.

pre— • before

    precocious – *ahead of one's time, talented.*
    prehistoric – *before recorded history.*
    prejudice – *bias, discrimination.*

Kent is a **precocious** child who continually impresses his teachers and fellow students.
The **prehistoric** cave paintings showed that early man had artistic tendencies.
The **prejudiced** landlord doesn't allow foreigners to live in his building.

pro— • forward

    proceed – *to move forward.*
    prospect – *view, outlook.*
    propulsion – *a force that moves something forward.*
    prognosis – *a prediction, a forecast.*

After the show, the audience quietly rose from their seats and **proceeded** to the exits.
Lyman became a rocket scientist and got a job at the Jet **Propulsion** Laboratory.
According to the doctor's **prognosis**, I'll be able to leave the hospital in a month.

pro— • in favor of
       • for

    pro-democracy – *supporting democracy.*
    pro-lifer – *a person who is against abortion.*
    pro-Jones – *on the side of Mr Jones, supporting Mr Jones.*

The Chinese army attacked the **pro-democracy** activists in Tienanmen Square.
The doctor was shot and killed by a **pro-lifer** in the parking lot of the abortion clinic.
The **pro-Jones** group gathered in front of city hall, chanting their candidate's name.

pseudo— • false

    pseudonym – *a fake name, an alias, a pen-name.*
    pseudo-intellectual – *a person who pretends to be smart.*
    pseudo-classic – *falsely classic, imitating the classics.*

He published his first two novels under the **pseudonym** Lewis Silvestri.
The professors avoid the **pseudo-intellectuals** who hang around by the staff lounge.

r—

re— • back
       • again

    reappear – *to come out again.*
    recover – *to get well.*
    reaction – *a response, a reflex.*
    reverse – *backwards.   to go backwards.*

After being lost for two weeks, our cat **reappeared** on our doorstep this morning.
He has been released from the hospital, but he hasn't yet **recovered** completely.
She was surprised that her statement caused such a strong **reaction**.

retro— • *backwards*
        retrospective – *contemplation of things past, a looking back.*
        retrorocket – *a rocket used to stop or reverse a missile.*
        retroactive – *taking effect from a previous date.*

The museum will host a month-long **retrospective** of the works of Kniel Spek.
The workers received a $3 per hour raise, **retroactive** to last April 1.

S—

se— • *away*
      • *without*
        secede – *to split off from.*
        segregate – *to separate, to keep apart.*
        secluded – *alone, closed off from.*

Separatists want Quebec to **secede** from Canada and became a separate state.
Racial **segregation** is illegal, although it is still practiced in some areas of the South.
We spent our vacation on a **secluded** beach on a tiny island off Okinawa.

semi— • *half*
        semicircle – *a half circle.*
        semiconscious – *not fully aware, not fully conscious.*
        semi-detached – *a house which is joined to another house.*

The pupils sat in a **semicircle** at the front of the class.
The accident victim was **semiconscious** when he was brought to the hospital.
After saving ten years for the down payment, they bought a **semi-detached** house.

sub— • *under*
      • *below*
        substandard – *of poor quality, below acceptable standards.*
        suburban – *outside the city.*
        submerge – *to put underwater.*
        submissive – *obedient, passive, weak.*
        subsequent – *happening afterwards, succeeding.*

We complained about the **substandard** service we received while staying at that hotel.
The myth of the **submissive** Japanese housewife is just that; a groundless fiction.
Phil was laid off from Chrysler, but he was **subsequently** hired by Ford.

super— • *above*
sur— • *beyond*
        supernatural – *unreal, miraculous, incredible.*
        supervisor – *a boss, an overseer.*
        supersede – *to replace, to displace.*
        surpass – *to exceed, to excel.*
        surprise – *to encounter suddenly, to cause to wonder.*
        surname – *last name, family name.*
        surplus – *extra, additional, an oversupply.*

I read a frightening book of ghost stories and other tales of the **supernatural**.

The typewriter was **superseded** by the computer.
We can get rid of the **surplus** goods by having a store-wide, week-long sale.

---

syn– • *similar*
sym– • *together*

    synthesize – *to combine, to produce by chemical reaction.*
    synchronize – *to set or occur at the same time.*
    sympathy – *understanding another's feelings, compassion.*

These paintings **synthesize** elements of aboriginal art with modern techniques.
Taka and I **synchronized** our watches to make sure that we would both arrive on time.
We would like to express our deepest **sympathy** on the death of your father.

---

t—

---

trans– • *across*

    transplant – *to replant, to plant in a different place.*
    transmit – *to send, to broadcast.*
    transformation – *a change, an alteration.*
    transcontinental – *across a continent.*

Once the plant has grown to about 30 centimeters, you should **transplant** it outside.
The internet has allowed us to **transmit** all sorts of information rapidly and cheaply.
He underwent a personal **transformation** after his near-death experience on Everest.

---

u—

---

ultra– • *beyond*
       • *extreme*

    ultramodern – *very new, very advanced.*
    ultraviolet – *beyond the violet in the spectrum of light rays.*
    ultrasonic – *pertaining to sounds beyond hearing range.*

This year's trade show features a wide selection of **ultramodern** equipment.
Be sure to protect your skin from exposure to the sun's **ultraviolet** rays.

---

un– • *not*

    unnatural – *artificial, abnormal.*
    unfamiliar – *not acquainted, different, unusual.*
    unrelated – *unconcerned, not connected.*
    ungrammatical – *grammatically incorrect or awkward.*

We enjoy traveling to exotic places and wandering through **unfamiliar** surroundings.
His comments were completely **unrelated** to the topic being discussed.
The other students could not understand most of Amin's **ungrammatical** babbling.

SUFFIXES

—a

—able · *can*
—ible · *possible*

portable – *carryable, movable.*
legible – *readable.*
interminable – *endless, continuous, very long.*
intolerable – *unbearable, painful.*
responsible – *trustworthy, dependable. guilty.*

You should rewrite these directions for me, because they are completely **illegible**.
We had to sit though the **interminable** discussion of the managers.
Chris is a **responsible** worker who will become a valuable asset for your company.

—ac · *pertaining to*
—ic · *of*

cardiac – *pertaining to the heart.*
aquatic – *pertaining to water.*
dramatic – *pertaining to drama. sensational, thrilling.*

Cardiac arrest is the medical term for a heart attack.
She will study botany, specializing in **aquatic** plants.
The stunt man made a **dramatic** leap from the bridge onto the car racing below.

—age · *(noun suffix)*

usage – *the way something is used, the degree of use.*
mileage – *distance measured in miles, usefulness.*
marriage – *the state of being married, a union.*

Andre has an extensive English vocabulary, but he has many problems with **usage**.
The opposition party got much **mileage** out of the prime minister's racist comments.
Their **marriage** broke up after the husband admitted his affair with the young model.

—al · *(adjective suffix)*

regional – *pertaining to a region.*
brutal – *merciless, cruel, very unpleasant.*
typical – *exemplary, ordinary.*

The people all speak the same language, but there are many **regional** dialects.
The **brutal** dictator was overthrown by a popular revolution.
On a **typical** workday, our manager will spend 12-14 hours at the office.

—al · *(noun suffix)*

refusal – *rejection, denial.*
approval – *agreement, support, recognition.*
renewal – *starting over, making something new again.*

The terrorists reasserted their **refusal** to free the hostages and surrender.
Brian never goes out drinking without the **approval** of his wife.
Trade between the countries has increased rapidly since the **renewal** of diplomatic ties.

–ance · *(noun suffix)*
–ence

reference – *talk about something, a thing which is referred to.*
disturbance – *an interruption, an outbreak of violence.*
difference – *the state of being different, contrast.*

The coach made no **reference** to my terrible error which led to their winning score.
The police were called in to settle the **disturbance**.
There are obviously some basic biological **differences** between men and women.

–ary · *as (adjective suffix)*
· *of*

momentary – *short, temporary, brief.*
customary – *usual, habitual, typical.*
revolutionary – *rebellious, radical.*

Even a **momentary** lapse of concentration can result in a complete loss of control.
In this country, it is **customary** to bring a gift when you visit people in their home.
The army was sent in to suppress the activities of the **revolutionary** organizations.

–ate · *(verb suffix)*

originate – *to start, to begin.*
substantiate – *to verify, to support with evidence.*
validate – *to make effective.*
devastate – *to destroy, to plunder.*

AIDS is said to have **originated** somewhere in Africa.
The discovery of water on Mars **validates** the theory that it could have sustained life.
Cities throughout the region were **devastated** by the major earthquake.

–ation · *(noun suffix)*
–tion

resignation – *retirement, the act of quitting.*
consideration – *thought, thoughtfulness, regard.*
intention – *plan, ambition, desire.*
hibernation – *the act of sleeping through the winter.*

The crowd of people cheered when the hated leader announced his **resignation**.
Please show **consideration** for others by not smoking during dinner.
The senator announced his **intention** to run for president in the next election.

–ative · *having a relation, a nature, or a tendency*
–tive

authoritative – *powerful, commanding, knowledgeable.*
decorative – *fancy, ornamental.*
formative – *pertaining to growth or development.*
instinctive – *natural, spontaneous, unconscious.*

With his **authoritative** presence, Mr Yoshida can change the atmosphere of a room.
He spent his **formative** years on a small farm, but moved to the city when he was 17.
Wayne Gretzky had an **instinctive** awareness of where the puck was at all times.

—c

—cle • *small*
—cule • *tiny*

    molecule – *a dot, a speck, a small amount.*
    minuscule – *very small.*
    corpuscle – *a blood cell.*

We studied the properties of water **molecules** in chemistry class today.
A **minuscule** amount of deadly poison was detected in the bottle of water.
My doctor said that the patient had a deficiency of red **corpuscles**.

—cracy • *government*
       • *rule*

    democracy – *government by the people.*
    aristocracy – *government by the nobility.*
    theocracy – *government based on a god or by priests.*

Somebody once said that **democracy** means government by the uneducated, while **aristocracy** means government by the badly educated.
Theocracy is government not by the indoctrinated, but by the *badly* indoctrinated.

—cy • *state of being*

    obstinacy – *stubbornness.*
    accuracy – *the state of being accurate.*
    intricacy – *the state of being detailed or complex.*

The psychiatrist helped me overcome my hostility and **obstinacy**.
Reporters questioned the **accuracy** of the numbers quoted by the Minister of Finance.
Tourists will be amazed at the **intricacy** of the design in the natives' artwork.

—e

—ee • *a person who is the object of an action*

    employee – *a person who is employed.*
    trainee – *a person who is being trained.*
    retiree – *a retired person.*

All **employees** will be laid off effective immediately.
As instructed, the naive **trainee** ran to the boiler room to get a bucket of steam.

—en • *(verb suffix)*

    hasten – *to hurry, to rush, to quicken.*
    deepen – *to make stronger, to make lower.*
    thicken – *to make thick, to become thick.*

Bob's constant smoking only **hastened** his death by cancer.
His interest in politics **deepened** after he read the president's biography.
Stir the sauce over low heat until it **thickens**.

–ent · *(adjective suffix)*
–ant · *characterized by*
  pleasant – *enjoyable, pleasing, charming.*
  excellent – *perfect, superb, extraordinary.*
  urgent – *critical, important, absolutely necessary.*

Thank you for a most **pleasant** and enjoyable evening.
You deserve to be promoted for the **excellent** work you've done to increase sales.
The accident victims are in **urgent** need of medical help.

–er · *a person who is the subject of an action*
–or
  employer – *a person who employs other people.*
  trainer – *a person who trains athletes or animals.*
  originator – *an inventor, a pioneer.*

We decided to ask our **employer** for a raise.
Behind every successful athlete is an inspiring, aggressive **trainer**.
Einstein was the **originator** of the general theory of relativity.

—f

–fic · *(adjective suffix)*
–ific · *making*
  terrific – *great, wonderful.*
  soporific – *sleep inducing.*
  horrific – *creating horror.*

We had a **terrific** time at the party last night.
Don't operate this machinery after taking drugs with **soporific** effects.
The mass murder was the most **horrific** crime in the history of the city.

–ful · *characterized by*
  · *with*
  peaceful – *calm, relaxed, non-violent.*
  skillful – *artistic, clever, resourceful.*
  delightful – *enjoyable, wonderful.*

They have negotiated a **peaceful** settlement to the dispute over ownership of the land.
He was a **skillful** politician who could charm almost anyone he met.
The children spent a **delightful** summer at the camp.

–ful · *full*
  spoonful – *an amount which fills one spoon.*
  mouthful – *an amount which fills a mouth, a lot of words.*
  earful – *a rebuke, a scolding.*

He takes his coffee with lots of cream and 3 **spoonfuls** of sugar.
The long name of the project is a real **mouthful** to say, so let's use an acronym.
I don't remember what Dad said when he scolded me, but I definitely got an **earful**.

–f y · (verb suffix)
–i f y · make

      petrify – *to turn into stone, to terrify.*
      magnify – *to enlarge, to make bigger.*
      intensify – *to strengthen, to increase.*

The children were **petrified** while the storm raged outside and shook the house.
Let's **magnify** the photo so that we can make out the details.
The music **intensified** in volume until we could not tolerate it any more.

—i

–i c · *as (adjective suffix)*
–i c a l · *like*

      basic – *fundamental, standard, lowest.*
      gigantic – *enormous, very large.*
      topical – *pertaining to current events.*
      economical – *thrifty, cheap to operate.*

The students first have to be taught **basic** grammar and vocabulary.
This news magazine has a reputation for covering **topical** issues.
Not only was my car inexpensive to buy, it's also **economical** to run.

–i l · *capable of (adjective suffix)*
–i l e · *pertaining to*

      civil – *pertaining to a country's citizens. polite but formal.*
      juvenile – *young, immature. youth.*
      puerile – *childish, very immature.*

The **civil** unrest of the 1960s resulted in drastic changes in American society.
The teenaged thief was sentenced to one year in a **juvenile** detention center.
None of Mr Hisamatsu's staff members could stand his **puerile** behavior.

–i s h · *as (adjective suffix)*
    · *like*

      bookish – *overly interested in books.*
      selfish – *concerned with only oneself.*
      foolish – *stupid, not wise.*
      nine-ish – *around nine o'clock.*

It's not worth your time trying to get to know such **bookish** people.
That man is so **selfish** and egotistical that he has very few friends.
We would be **foolish** to try to drive across Canada in this old beat-up Ford.

–i s m · *theory*
    · *doctrine*
    · *practice*

      Buddhism – *belief in the teachings of Buddha.*
      communism – *Marxism.*
      rationalism – *belief in reason.*

The tenets of **Buddhism** are virtually unknown in the west.

Hardline **Communism** still thrives in North Korea and Cuba.
The emphasis on **rationalism** in western thought has left many in a spiritual void.

–ist   • *doer*
            • *practitioner*
                    humorist – *a person who provides humor.*
                    specialist – *a person who engages in a special field.*
                    optimist – *a person who is hopeful.*

Charles Schulz was one of the most beloved **humorists** of all time.
My doctor advised me to see a **specialist**.
She is a true **optimist** whose cheerful manner affects everyone she meets.

–itis   • *inflammatory disease*
            • *bad condition* (colloquial)
                    tonsillitis – *inflammation of the tonsils.*
                    bronchitis – *inflammation of the bronchial tubes.*
                    study-itis – *bad condition due to too much studying.*
                    golf-itis – *bad condition due to too much golf.*

The child had to go to the hospital for an operation because he had **tonsillitis**.
Your **bronchitis** will be aggravated if you keep smoking.
The sales manager had to take a sick-day due to a severe case of **golf-itis**.

–ity   • *condition*
            • *quality*
                    ability – *skill, aptitude.*
                    minority – *a number which is less than half the total.*
                    stability – *balance, firmness, strength.*
                    sagacity – *wisdom.*
                    vocab-ability – *skillful use of a wide range of words.*

Meg has the desire and motivation to be a tennis star, but she doesn't have the **ability**.
The **minority** government accomplished very little due its lack of **stability**.
The interviewer was impressed by the **sagacity** of the great writer.

–ive   • *(adjective suffix)*
            • *characterized by*
                    attractive – *pretty, beautiful, alluring.*
                    preventive – *precautionary, designed to safeguard.*
                    curative – *helping to cure, corrective.*
                    possessive – *greedy, selfish.*

Beautiful women are not always the most **attractive** women.
Many doctors now emphasize **preventive** medicine over **curative** medicine.
She had a hard time breaking off from her boyfriend because he was very **possessive**.

–ize   • *do (verb suffix)*
            • *make*
                    victimize – *to make a victim, to injure.*
                    rationalize – *to justify, to explain, to streamline.*
                    harmonize – *to make peaceful, to fit well together.*
                    legalize – *to make legal.*
                    civilize – *to educate, to enlighten, to refine.*

Some illicit drugs should be **legalized** for medical use.

—l

—less · without
· not

worthless – *cheap, inferior, having no value.*
restless – *unsettled, uncomfortable, anxious.*
timeless – *permanent, eternal.*

We made over $100 selling all that **worthless** junk at our garage sale.
The crowd became **restless** while waiting for the band to appear on stage.
The simple beauty of those designs gives them a **timeless** appeal.

—like · *(adjective suffix)*
· *similar*

lifelike – *real-looking, realistic.*
warlike – *hostile, belligerent, aggressive.*
businesslike – *serious, efficient, practical.*

Tourists flock to the wax museum to see the **lifelike** figures of famous people.
Historians believe that the ancient race of people had a **warlike** society.
Greg's **businesslike** attitude makes him the ideal candidate for the manager's post.

—ly · *as (adjective suffix)*
· *like*

worldly – *experienced, sophisticated, not spiritual.*
orderly – *controlled, systematic, steady.*
costly – *expensive.*

The high school teacher in the rural town was seen as a **worldly** man.
The students were told to leave the auditorium in an **orderly** manner.
My car needs some **costly** repairs, so I'll be cycling until I can save a bit of money.

—m

—ment · *(noun suffix)*

argument – *a debate, a quarrel.*
refreshment – *a drink or bit of food to revitalize someone.*
installment – *a partial payment.*

Mr and Mrs Sakurai got into a big **argument** last night about her spending habits.
Dinner will not be served, but some **refreshments** will be provided during the break.
You will have to repay the loan in monthly **installments** over a period of two years.

—n

—ness · condition
· quality

sadness – *suffering, sorrow, distress.*
foolishness – *nonsense, craziness.*
darkness – *the state of being dark.*

After the death of her child, she was overcome with great **sadness**.
The teacher scolded the students for their utter **foolishness**.
The city was plunged into **darkness** when the electric company went on strike.

—o

—ous · (adjective suffix)
—ious · like
—ose · full of

nervous – *uneasy, tense, sensitive.*
courageous – *brave, fearless.*
insidious – *treacherous, seductive, harmful.*
verbose – *wordy, talkative.*

The young actor was very **nervous** before his stage debut.
The soldiers were praised for their **courageous** fight against the large army.
Some citizens warned of the possible **insidious** effects of the segregationist laws.

—s

—sion · (noun suffix)
—tion

confusion – *commotion, chaos, disorder.*
intention – *plan, goal.*
invasion – *attack, penetration, intrusion.*

After the accident, there was much **confusion** until the police came.
The star pitcher said he had no **intentions** of retiring in the near future.
Your reading of my personal diary was an **invasion** of my privacy.

—u

—ure · (noun suffix)

failure – *downfall, lack of success.*
pressure – *a strong force, stress.*
mixture – *a blend, a variety, a combination.*
censure – *disapproval, condemnation. to disapprove.*

The president lost the election because of his **failure** to stimulate the economy.
Those children view their father with a **mixture** of admiration and fear.
The student newspaper editors defied the **censure** of the university administration.

—y

—y • *(adjective suffix)*
   wavy – *having waves.*
   rainy – *having lots of rain.*
   sleepy – *tired, wanting to sleep.*

Karen is blessed with naturally **wavy** hair.
The weatherman said that we could expect a few **rainy** days.
You should put the children to bed soon. They seem quite **sleepy**.

—y • *(noun suffix)*
   flattery – *compliment, praise, insincere praise.*
   summary – *a condensed statement.*
   symmetry – *balance, harmony.*

Be careful that you aren't deceived by his **flattery**.
I didn't have time to read the entire report, so I just read the **summary**.
Each snowflake is unique, but all are characterized by a beautiful **symmetry**.

NUMBERS

mono– · *1*
uni– · *one*

monotonous – *dull, boring, having an unvaried sound.*
monorail – *a railway with one rail.*
monomaniac – *a person obsessed with one thing.*
uniform – *unvarying, having a single form or pattern.*
unite – *to join, to combine.*
unify – *to combine, to integrate.*
unilateral – *one-sided, pertaining to only one side.*

This job is so **monotonous**. I'm going to quit and find a more interesting one.
Travelers can get from downtown to the airport in 15 minutes on the new **monorail**.
The government made a **unilateral** decision to destroy its nuclear arsenal.

bi– · *2*
di– · *two*
du–
doubl–
dupl–

biennial – *every two years.*
bilateral – *2-sided.*
bilingual – *able to speak two languages.*
binary – *consisting of two parts or elements.*
divide – *to split, to separate into two parts.*
dichotomy – *division into two separate groups.*
dioxide – *an oxide with two oxygen atoms per molecule.*
duo – *a pair, a couple.*
double – *twice as much.*
duet – *a musical composition for two people.*
duplicate – *to copy. a copy.*

The voice teacher and her student sang a **duet** at the music festival.
You must make a **duplicate** of this form and sign both copies.
They bought the other half of the **duplex** and **doubled** their living area.

tri– · *3*
· *three*

tripod – *a 3-legged stand for a camera or telescope.*
triumvirate – *a group of three leaders.*
trilogy – *a series of three books or plays.*

The photographer affixed his camera to the **tripod**.
That growing company is run by a **triumvirate** of young men with MBAs.
Many readers said that the second and third books of the **trilogy** were not very good.

quart– · *4*
quad– · *four*
tetra–

quarter – *one-fourth, 25 cents.*
quartet – *a musical group with four people.*
quadrangle – *an area with four sides.*
quart – *one-fourth of a gallon.*
quadruped – *a 4-legged animal.*
tetrapod – *an object with four nodes or feet.*
tetralogy – *a series of four related dramas or novels.*

The bride and groom hired a string **quartet** to play at their wedding ceremony.
The protesters gathered in the **quadrangle** in the center of campus.
Parts of the Japanese coast are lined with large, ugly, concrete **tetrapods**.

---

pent– · *5*
quint– · *five*

pentagon – *a 5-sided figure, a 5-angled figure.*
pentathlon – *an athletic competition comprising five events.*
quintuplets – *five babies born together.*
quintet – *a musical group of five people.*
quintessential – *pure and concentrated in nature, typical.*

The **Pentagon** is the five-sided headquarters of the US Defense Department.
The woman gave birth to **quintuplets** after taking fertility drugs.
Tokyo is a multicultural city, but Kyoto remains the **quintessential** Japanese city.

---

hexa– · *6*
sexa– · *six*

hexagon – *a 6-sided figure.*
sextuplets – *six babies born together.*
sexagenarian – *a person in his 60s.*

The new company logo is a **hexagon** with a slash through it.
The woman gave birth to **sextuplets** after taking more fertility drugs.
Tony was a real Don Juan who had affairs even after he became a **sexagenarian**.

---

hept– · *7*
sept– · *seven*

septilateral – *a 7-sided figure.*
September – *originally the 7th month (now the 9th month).*
septuagenarian – *a person in his 70s.*
heptagon – *a 7-sided figure.*

It was hard for Tony to seduce women when he was a **septuagenarian**.
Most graphic designers have never seen or drawn a **heptagon**, let alone used the word.

oct– • *8*
  • *eight*

> **octopus** – *an 8-legged creature.*
> **octave** – *a series of eight musical notes.*
> **octogenarian** – *a person in his 80s.*
> **October** – *originally the 8th month (now the 10th).*

The **octopus** is a strange-looking – and *not* very tasty – marine creature.
The mayor of the town sent a congratulatory birthday message to the **octogenarian**.

nov– • *9*
non– • *nine*

> **nonagon** – *a 9-sided figure.*
> **nonagenarian** – *a person in his 90s.*
> **November** – *originally the 9th month (now the 11th).*

The **nonagenarian** had Alzheimer's, so he asked for help with an assisted suicide.
A **nonagon** is an asymmetrical figure – or it would be if anyone ever drew one.

dec– • *10*
  • *ten*

> **decade** – *ten years.*
> **decathlon** – *a series of ten athletic events.*
> **December** – *originally the 10th month (now the 12th).*
> **decimate** – *to destroy, to reduce in size greatly (by 10%).*

There was much optimism during the first **decade** of the new century.
Bruce was a great athlete who excelled in each sport of the **decathlon**.
The wildlife in the area was **decimated** by pollution from the chemical factory.

cent– • *100*
  • *one hundred*

> **centimeter** – $^1/_{100th}$ *of a meter.*
> **century** – *one hundred years.*
> **bicentennial** – *200th anniversary.*
> **fifty per cent** – *50 out of 100, 50%.*
> **centigrade** – *a scale for measuring heat, from 0 to 100.*

America celebrated its **bicentennial** in 1976.
The **centigrade** scale is easier to understand than the Fahrenheit scale.

milli– • *1000*
  • *one thousand*

> **millimeter** – $^1/_{1000th}$ *of a meter.*
> **millennium** – *a thousand years.*
> **million** – *1,000,000.*
> **millipede** – *a small bug with many feet.*

The glass slide is only 2 **millimeters** thick.
It seemed sensible to celebrate the new **millennium** again on December 31, 2000.
If you hope to make **millions** of dollars, self-publishing a book ain't the way to do it.

INDEX

This index contains only the meanings of the roots presented in this book. It does not contain the roots, the sample words, their definitions, or words that may appear in the model sentences.

a

above – **22, 66**
across – **57, 67**
act – **1, 15**
add – **4**
after – **58, 64**
again – **65**
against – **55, 56, 56, 63**
age – **14**
agree – **21**
all – **63**
around – **8, 64**
artistry – **46**
as – **69, 72, 72, 74**
ask – **36, 40, 40**
at – **53**
attention – **10**
attract – **49**
away – **53, 57, 57, 66**

b

back – **65**
backwards – **66**
bad – **61**
bad condition – **73**
before – **54, 65**
being (state of ...) – **70**
believe – **10**
below – **66**
bend – **9, 16, 37, 43**
beside – **64**
best – **33**
between – **28, 60**
better – **28**
beyond – **22, 59, 64, 66, 67**
big – **61, 61**
birth – **31**
bitter – **1**
blame – **10**
body – **9**

boil – **15**
book – **5, 25**
both – **54**
bottom – **18**
break – **18, 41**
breath – **45**
bring – **13, 15**
brother – **18**
build – **46**
burn – **16**

c

calculate – **39**
call – **8, 51**
can – **68**
capable of – **72**
care – **10**
carry – **15, 38**
center – **7**
chance – **17**
change – **2, 31, 50**
characterized by – **71, ...**
 ... **71, 73**
chief – **55**
child – **35**
choose – **24**
citizen – **8**
city – **38, 49**
class – **19**
clear – **8**
climb – **41**
close – **8**
color – **7**
come – **50**
companion – **43**
completely – **64**
condition – **73, 75**
connect – **26**
conquer – **51**
contain – **6**

continue – **43**
correct – **34**
cry out – **8**
crazed person – **28**
cut – **7, 42**

d

day – **12, 23**
death – **31**
deceive – **15**
degree – **20**
deny – **32**
different – **59**
difficult – **57**
disease – **73**
distant – **47**
do – **55, 73**
doctrine – **72**
doer – **73**
down – **56, 57**

e

earth – **19, 48**
empty – **49**
end – **16, 48**
enthusiasm – **27**
equal – **14, 34**
era – **14**
escape – **18**
extend – **47**
extreme – **67**

f

face – **15, 18**
faith – **16**
fall – **5, 24**
false – **65**
far – **47**
father – **35**

81

faulty – **57**
favor (in ... of) – **65**
favorable – **37**
fear – **36**
feel – **14, 42**
feeling – **34**
field – **1**
fight – **1**
figure – **17**
fire – **6, 16**
first – **39, 55**
flee – **18**
flow – **11, 17**
flock – **20**
fold – **37, 43**
follow – **43**
foot – **35**
for – **65**
force – **35**
fore – **18**
form – **31**
former – **59**
forward – **54, 65**
free – **26**
friendship – **2**
from – **53, 55, 58**
front – **59**
full – **37, 71**
full of – **75**
furnish – **34**

g

give – **11**
go – **6, 20, 22**
good – **4, 58**
god – **48**
govern – **13**
government – **3, 70**
great – **61, 61**
group – **20**
grow – **10**
guest – **22**

h

half – **59, 66**
hand – **27**

hang down – **35**
hard – **13**
hate – **62**
head – **5**
hear – **4**
heart – **9**
heat – **48**
heavy – **20**
herd – **20**
hold – **47**
holy – **41, 41**
host – **22**
hot – **15**
huge – **61**
human – **3, 21**

i

in – **60**
increase – **4**
inflammatory disease – **73**

j

join – **23**
judge – **3**

k

keep – **43**
kill – **7**
kind – **19**
know – **9, 19, 41**

l

land – **48**
language – **26**
large – **61, 61**
lasting – **13**
laugh – **40**
law – **23, 25**
lead – **1, 13**
leaf – **17**
lean – **9**
learn – **9**
leave out – **26**
less – **22**
life – **2, 5, 51**

lift – **25**
light – **25**
light – **27, 37**
like – **72, 72, 74, 75**
limit – **16**
lion – **25**
live – **21**
love – **2, 36**
loosen – **44**
look – **45**
luck – **17**
lunatic – **28**

m

madness – **27**
make – **15, 55, 58, 72, 73**
making – **71**
man – **21**
manner – **30**
many – **38, 62, 64**
mark – **45**
marriage – **19**
material – **37**
measure – **29**
meat – **6**
melt – **19**
middle – **7, 28**
mind – **2, 9, 29, 39**
model – **17**
mother – **28**
move – **6, 30**
much – **38, 62, 64**
much (too ...) – **64**

n

name – **32**
narrow – **47**
nature – **37, 69**
new – **33, 63**
not – **53, 57, 60, 63, . . .**
. . . **67, 74**
nothing – **32**
nourish – **33**

o

of – **68, 69**
off – **55**
omit – **26**
on – **58**
one – **44**
operate – **15**
opposed to – **55**
opposing – **56**
opposite – **57**
other – **2, 59**
out – **58**
outside – **59**
over – **58**
owe – **11**

p

pay – **29**
peace – **34**
people – **11, 38**
perceive – **14**
person (crazed) – **28**
person – **70, 71**
pertaining to – **68, 72**
place – **26, 38**
pleasing – **20**
pleasant – **37**
possible – **68**
pour – **19**
power – **13, 39**
practice – **72**
practitioner – **73**
previous – **59**
prick – **45**
pull – **49**
push – **35, 39**
put – **38**

q

quality – **73, 75**

r

race – **19**
read – **25**

relation – **69**
remember – **29**
remind – **30**
reside – **21**
reverse – **55**
right – **23, 40**
rise – **46**
rock – **36**
roll – **52**
rule – **3, 13, 70**
run – **11**

s

same – **60**
say – **12**
sea – **28**
secret – **10**
see – **51**
seek – **36, 40**
self – **13, 55**
send – **30**
sense – **42**
separate – **7**
serve – **43**
settle – **42**
shape – **15, 17, 31, 37**
sharp – **1**
shine – **6**
ship – **32**
short – **5**
shut – **8**
side – **24**
similar – **67, 74**
sister – **44**
sit – **42**
skill – **46**
skin – **12**
sleep – **44**
slip – **24**
small – **29, 62, 70**
small (very ...) – **62**
soul – **2**
sound – **36, 44**
speak – **51**
speech – **27, 36**
speed – **6**
spirit – **2, 45**

stand – **45**
stage – **20**
star – **4**
state of being – **70**
stick – **21**
stone – **36**
straight – **34, 40**
strength – **13**
stretch – **47**
strong – **16, 17, 49**
study – **27**
suffer – **1**
suffering – **34**
sun – **21**
support – **16**
swear – **23**

t

take – **6**
teach – **12**
tell – **32**
tendency – **69**
thankful – **20**
theory – **72**
thin – **47**
think – **39, 42**
through – **57, 64**
throw – **23**
tie – **26, 45**
tight – **45**
time – **7, 14, 47**
tiny – **29, 62, 70**
to – **54, 63**
together – **56, 67**
tongue – **26**
too much – **22, 64**
tooth – **12**
touch – **46**
toward – **53, 60, 63**
trade – **29**
trip – **22**
true – **50**
trust – **10, 16**
turn – **16, 50**
twist – **49**

u

under – **22, 66**
unfortunate – **30**
unite – **23**
universe – **10**
upon – **60**
urge – **1**

v

valuable – **49**
very big – **61**
very small – **62**
view – **42**
vision – **33**
vow – **23**

w

walk – **2**
wall – **31**
wander – **14**
war – **4**
warn – **30**
watch – **42**
water – **3, 22**
way – **30, 50**
will – **52**
wise – **44**
wish – **52**
with – **56, 71**
within – **61**
without – **53, 60, 66, 74**
witness – **48**
word – **27, 50**
work – **14, 24, 33**
world – **10**
wretched – **30**
write – **42**
writing – **20**
wrong – **15, 61, 62**

y

year – **3**
young – **24**